Edinburgh Bilingual Library (12)

Edinburgh Bilingual Library (12)

AUSIAS MARCH
Selected Poems

Edited and Translated by
ARTHUR TERRY
Professor of Literature
University of Essex

University of Texas Press,
Austin

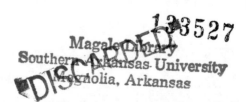

International Standard Book Number 0-292-70323-6 (cloth);
0-292-70324-4 (paper)
Library of Congress Catalog Card Number 76-29519
Copyright © 1976 by Arthur Terry
Set in 10/11 'Monotype' Barbou
and printed in Great Britain by
W & J Mackay Limited, Chatham

Edinburgh Bilingual Library

FOREWORD

An imperfect knowledge of a language need be no bar to reading a work written in it if there is a good translation to help. This Library may aid those who have a wide-ranging and adventurous interest in literature to jump the hurdles of language and thus do something to help break down the barriers of specialization. That it may be helpful for courses in Comparative Literature is our hope, but not our main aim. We wish to appeal to a wider audience: first to the cultivated, serious reader of literature who is not content to remain within the English language, secondly to university students and teachers of English and of Modern Languages by inviting them to throw from outside some new light on, perhaps even discover different values in, their particular fields of specialization.

The languages represented will be French (with Provençal), German, Italian, Portuguese, Spanish (with Catalan), and Medieval and Renaissance Latin. The translations will not be 'cribs' but good literature worth publishing in its own right. Verse will generally be translated into verse, except where the unfamiliarity of the language for most readers (Provençal, Catalan, Old French, Old High German) may make a more literal prose rendering advisable. In the majority of cases the Introductions will present up-to-date assessments of each author or work, or original interpretations on a scholarly level. Works already accessible in translation will be included only when we think we can offer a new translation of special excellence or when we wish to relate it to another volume in the series.

Contents

Ausias March

INTRODUCTION

A bilingual anthology of the poetry of Ausias March (1397–1459) seems justified for several reasons. In the first place, because he is unquestionably a major writer, the finest poet working anywhere in Europe between Chaucer and Villon —that is to say, in the first half of the fifteenth century. Secondly, because he comes at an important stage in the courtly tradition which is one of the strongest links between medieval and Renaissance poetry, and because he bears a subtle and at times ambivalent relation to that tradition. And lastly, since, as I shall try to explain, the language in which he writes—Catalan—is crucial to his whole situation as a poet; so much so that, if we understand the reasons for this, we shall have begun to realize why an exceptionally gifted fifteenth-century poet should have reacted to the tradition as he did.

This last point is probably the best one to start from, and it means looking back for a moment over the earlier history of medieval Catalan verse. The first thing to notice is how different this is from the development of early Catalan prose. There, one has a rich and accomplished body of literature from the late thirteenth century onwards—chronicles, fables, moral and religious writing—culminating in a brilliant group of humanistic writers, most of whom were still alive at the time Ausias March was born.

On the other hand, the language of all serious poetry written in Catalonia from the early thirteenth century to the time of Ausias March is Provençal. At the beginning of the period, this seems natural enough: cultural and political links between Catalonia and the south of France are so strong that the same troubadours move freely over the whole area, and a poet from Barcelona or Girona feels himself as closely involved in the dominant tradition as one from Narbonne or Montpellier. After 1213, when King Peter I of Aragon is killed at the battle of Muret, fighting for the Albigensians against Simon de Montfort, the situation changes. The links between Catalonia and Provence are weakened, as is the power of the small courts in the south of France where troubadour poetry had flourished. As a result, the centre of the whole tradition shifts to Catalonia, and it is in the second half of the thirteenth century that one finds the last and most brilliant of the Catalan troubadours, Cerverí de Girona (d. *post* 1282). Even after the break with the south of France, it seems fairly natural that troubadour poetry should continue to be composed in Catalonia: it is a kind of poetry that tends to flourish best in the atmosphere of small courts, and the courts of thirteenth-century Catalonia are not so very different from those of Provence. The turning-point comes in the fourteenth century. A little before this, in the 1270s, there had emerged one of the greatest figures in the whole of Catalan literature, the religious writer and visionary Ramon Llull (1233–1316). It is Llull who, almost single-handed, establishes Catalan as the standard medium for prose, to such effect that there is no later medieval Catalan prose-writer who equals the richness and absolute assurance of his language. Llull was also a poet of some originality: in his poetry, which is entirely religious, and in some of his mystical prose, he quite clearly takes over certain themes and images from secular troubadour verse and uses them for his own ends. Here at least, then, we have the beginnings of a radically different kind of poetry which seems to be moving on from the existing tradition. Yet, in his poetry, Llull fails to do precisely what he had done so effectively in his prose: instead of using the Catalan language, he continues to write his verse in Provençal; in other words, instead of re-shaping the medium entirely, he continues to feel the weight of troubadour poetry, even though his poetic aims are quite different.

There seems little doubt that if Llull had made the leap into Catalan at this point, the subsequent history of Catalan poetry would have been very different. What happened instead is much less remarkable. To put it briefly, the troubadour tradition was prolonged throughout the fourteenth century as a consciously artificial mode of composition, which became increasingly separated from the true sources of Catalan culture. This process has a parallel in the south of France. Just as the first organization of troubadour poets—the *Sobregaia Companhia dels Set Trobadors*—was set up at Toulouse in 1323, with a complicated apparatus of rules and prizes, so seventy years later, in 1393, the *Consistori de la Gaia Ciència* was established at Barcelona, with exactly the same intentions. The effect of this was simply to confirm the general stagnation of serious poetry in Catalonia which had come about earlier in the fourteenth century. Clearly, there is nothing to compare here with the way in which Italian poetry was able to develop through the *stil nuovo* to Dante and Petrarch, nor to the way in which French poets like Machaut or Alain Chartier were able to transform older techniques and forms. This, then, is the situation in Catalan poetry around 1400: Provençal is still being maintained, though with increasing difficulty, as an artificial poetic language, though against this one has to set the rather timid beginnings of a satirical poetry in Catalan. And, curiously enough, the courtly love tradition itself, after remaining sterile for over a century, is going through a successful minor revival, partly through Italian influence, in the work of poets like Gilabert de Próxita, Melcior Guables and Andreu Febrer (*c.* 1375–*c.* 1444), one of the earliest translators of the *Divine Comedy*.

It would be easy to say at this point that the appearance of Ausias March changed everything. Yet this would not be quite true, and it would be particularly unjust to one excellent minor poet, Jordi de Sant Jordi, who died in 1425, still in his twenties. Jordi de Sant Jordi was a member of the Valencian nobility, like Ausias March himself, whom he knew. Unlike the more conventional poets of the time, he is capable of writing love poems which are both moving and elegantly phrased—so much so that, with his example before one, it is tempting to say that all the tradition needed, even at this late stage, was a poet of sufficient talent and personality. How Jordi de Sant Jordi might have developed had he lived longer, one can only guess: the poems he managed to write show him still using a slightly Catalanized Provençal, still moving very consciously within the orbit of troubadour poetry, though with occasional touches which suggest that he had read

Petrarch. Yet, good as they are, his poems show no real questioning of the earlier tradition, and their more pessimistic moments are a long way from the tormented introspection of Ausias March.

What Ausias March has to offer, roughly speaking, is not so much an alternative tradition as a way out of the existing one, above all in the direction I have just mentioned, of introspection and self-awareness. And connected with this is the fact that he is the first poet to write entirely in Catalan. If we take this fact for what it is—as something that determines the actual tone and vocabulary of his poems—the reason for his choice seems obvious: the independence of mind that shows through all his best writing seems to demand a language that will remove his poetry at one stroke from the conventional associations of Provençal.

Oddly enough, his relation to the tradition is echoed in the facts of his life. As is often the case with medieval poets, there is a baffling gap between the nature of the poetry and the biographical facts that have survived. Yet it is surely curious that both the father and uncle of Ausias March were respectable, if dull, minor poets, and that his uncle, Jaume March, was one of the people entrusted by royal command with drawing up the statutes of the *Consistori de la Gaia Ciència* in 1393. When he comes to write his own poetry, Ausias March is reacting very forcefully to the largely sterile tradition that these older poets represent. Apart from this, his life seems in no way different from that of dozens of his contemporaries who wrote no poetry. His family belonged to the minor Valencian nobility, though in fact it had only been raised to noble status in 1360; certainly, there are moments in his poems when one detects a lack of confidence in his social rank, which contrasts very noticeably with the absolute assurance of a hereditary aristocrat like Jordi de Sant Jordi. Like Jordi de Sant Jordi, however, he took part in the wars in Naples, Sicily and North Africa in the early 1420s, and in 1425 was singled out for special praise by King Alfonso IV of Aragon, who granted him various privileges in connection with the family estates in Valencia. At that point he seems to have retired permanently from the military life, and not long afterwards he probably wrote his first poems. In his later years, we catch glimpses of him engaged in the typical activities of a fifteenth-century squire: fighting lawsuits with rich neighbours, administering justice and raising falcons for the king. In 1437, when he was about forty, he married for the first time: his wife was the sister of Joanot Martorell (*c.*1410–68), the author of the greatest and most original of the novels of chivalry, *Tirant lo Blanc*. Two years later, she died, and in 1443 he married again. This new marriage lasted eleven years, in the course of which Ausias March took up residence in the city of Valencia. Then, in 1454, his second wife died, and it is possible that her death is related to some of his most moving poems. Ausias March himself survived her by five years, leaving no legitimate children, though several illegitimate ones are mentioned in his will.

Most of this would be of very little interest if it were not for the poems. It is scarcely an exaggeration to say that the blurred impression that comes from the biographical facts pales into insignificance beside the very strong sense of personality that runs through the poetry. The poet who can write at the climax of one of his most powerful poems 'Io só aquest que em dic Ausias March' [I am this man who is called Ausias March] needs no biographer to bring out his individuality, and, even at their most abstract, his poems give the impression of a living person who is anxiously debating matters that deeply concern him.

Ausias March has often been described as a courtly love poet. If one thinks of the high proportion of love poems in his work (something like three-quarters of a total of 128 poems), this would seem perfectly justified: a great deal of this poetry *is* related to the courtly tradition, either directly or by contrast. But, taking his work as a whole, there is a good case for calling it 'moral poetry', rather than simply 'love poetry'. A few poems, in fact, are clearly moral poems, and not love poems at all; these are generally poems that meditate philosophically on questions like the nature of virtue and goodness, often in a fairly predictable way. Much more important than these are the poems that centre on death. There are half-a-dozen of these, and there is little doubt that they represent Ausias March's supreme achievement. Moreover, all these poems are concerned, not merely with death in a general way, but with the death of a particular person, a woman whom the poet has loved in the fullest possible sense, and inevitably they lead him to thoughts about his own death. This is where Ausias March leaves the courtly love tradition furthest behind, and in talking about these poems, the critic must do the same. However, before we come to them, there is, as I have suggested, a considerable body of love poetry, and here, if we know anything about earlier courtly love poetry, we shall find that, at least for part of the time, we are on familiar ground.

There is one misconception which is still fairly general among critics of Ausias March, and which needs to be cleared out of the way before we look at any of the poems in detail. This is the notion that all his love poems are addressed to a single woman. This, in turn, has led to the idea that Ausias March's love poetry as a whole forms a single *canzoniere* in the manner of Petrarch, that he is the poet of the one woman he actually names—Teresa—in the sense that Petrarch is the poet of Laura. Such a misunderstanding is largely the fault of certain nineteenth-century critics, but, though it dies hard, it scarcely stands up to a reading of the poems. If one looks at these, one finds that nearly all of them are addressed to a particular woman, and that the woman in question is referred to in the final *envoi* by means of a pseudonym, or *senyal*. This, of course, is a standard troubadour device which, apart from anything else, emphasizes the private nature of the poem, the need for secrecy which is constantly stressed in the theory of courtly love. In the poems of Ausias March, there are two chief pseudonyms and a number of less important ones: the first is 'Llir entre cards'—'Lily among thorns'—a phrase that comes from the *Song of Solomon*, and the second is 'Plena de seny': literally, 'Full of sense', though the word *seny* has something of the overtones it possesses in modern Catalan— not merely 'common sense', but a more intellectual power, the idea of intelligence.

The poems, as they are printed in the standard editions of Ausias March, do not follow any obvious order. In particular, there is no attempt to group the nineteen poems addressed to 'Plena de seny' or the thirty-five poems addressed to 'Llir entre cards', and the same is true of the poems that use other pseudonyms. Yet if one picks out each set of poems and reads it as a cycle, some striking differences emerge. In the 'Plena de seny' cycle, for instance, one cannot help noticing

how the woman is constantly referred to as 'aimia' [beloved],
a term that is not used in the 'Llir entre cards' poems; also,
in the first cycle, there is an insistence on the woman's
relative lack of love, compared with the poet. There are also
touches that directly suggest the courtly love tradition, like
the references to the malicious slanderers, the *lozengiers*; and
at times, there are even derogatory remarks about the woman,
something that is quite lacking in the other cycle. In the 'Llir
entre cards' poems, on the other hand, we are told the name
of the woman—Teresa—, who is described physically, in
terms that seem to go beyond the conventional type of por-
trait; we also learn that she is married, with children, that she
willingly receives the poems addressed to her, and that she
takes pleasure in the poet's conversation and in the fact that
he celebrates her in his poems. Moreover, though both cycles
refer to death, this is a much more central theme in the 'Llir
entre cards' poems, which also refer to the poet's timidity and
consequent inability to put his feelings into words, to the
divine nature of the woman, and to the poet's shame at his
previous love affairs. There are other minor differences: but
these are enough to suggest that the two cycles are addressed
to different women, and it seems likely that the same is true
of the other, shorter cycles.

One of the best of the poems addressed to 'Llir entre cards'
begins as follows:

Lleixant a part l'estil dels trobadors
qui, per escalf, traspassen veritat,
e sostraent mon voler afectat
perquè no em torb, diré el que trob en vós.
Tot mon parlar als qui no us hauran vista
res no valdrà, car fe no hi donaran,
e los veents que dins vós no veuran,
en creure a mi, llur arma serà trista...

[Leaving aside the manner of the troubadours, who,
carried away by passion, exceed the truth, and restraining
my own amorous desire so that it does not distract me, I
shall say what I find in you. All my speech will be in vain
to those who have not seen you, for they will not believe
it; and those who see you, if they cannot see within, will
be sad at heart when they believe me...]

The greater part of this poem is concerned with praising the woman. The strategy by which this is done is rather like that of Mark Antony's funeral oration in Shakespeare's *Julius Caesar*: by affecting not to use rhetoric, what is said is made all the more persuasive. Hence the opening reference to the troubadours. It is difficult to know just how much weight to attach to this: some critics have seen these lines as a general condemnation of troubadour poetry on the grounds of insincerity. Yet this needs some qualification: it is likely, for instance, that when Ausias March writes the word *estil*, he means simply 'manner' or 'custom', rather than 'style' in a more literary sense, as if he were saying: 'We all know that troubadours are inclined to exaggerate; what I am about to say is the plain truth'. At the same time, we must not underestimate this opening gesture: there can be no question that, taking his poems as a whole, the kind of introspection they contain goes much deeper than anything one finds in the troubadours, and that this depth depends to a great extent on not idealizing their subject. What one does find quite often in Ausias March is a pride in the fact that he is a master— perhaps even the only master—in the art of love, so that from time to time he speaks as an expert addressing a select band of disciples. There is a hint of this in the present poem, which insists a good deal on the inaccurate judgements of those who only see the woman's surface qualities, though at one point, rather untypically, he associates *himself* with the general inarticulateness: 'Tots som grossers...' [We are all coarse...].

There is perhaps less to say about the actual praise of the lady. Though the whole poem is beautifully integrated, there are a number of statements that could be paralleled from earlier poetry. What is striking, however, is the way in which the praise is never allowed to get out of hand: we are reminded at various moments that, though the woman is a model of perfection, she is still a human being, and never more so than when she is told: 'verge no sou perquè Déu ne volc casta' [you are no virgin, since God wished you to bear offspring]. It is also clear that the praise is not confined to physical qualities, though these are obviously allowed for. This, in a way, is the whole point of the poem: in distinguishing between the trained observers and the less perceptive ones, the poet is distinguishing between different aspects of the woman: there is 'colour', but there is also 'texture'; there is 'stance' or 'manner of bearing', but there is also 'gesture'—something much more subtle and difficult to interpret.

This, for Ausias March, is a relatively serene poem. Though it is not certain that he ever read Dante, the closing lines convey something of the sense of miracle one finds in the *Vita Nuova*, in a poem like 'Tanto gentile e tan honesta pare…'. But if one wants to suggest the range of these poems, one only has to turn to those which attempt to deal with the prospect of death, like the one which begins: 'Quins tans segurs consells vas encercant…' [What certain guidance do you seek…] (xi). This poem, admittedly, is less perfect than the previous one: there is something of a break after the third stanza, in that the allegory of the first part comes to an end, and the poet begins to talk about himself in a more leisurely way. But this is only a minor defect, and the last four lines are just as intense in their way as the beginning. If one is used to reading Catalan poetry, one is particularly aware, in a poem like this, of the way in which the sound echoes the sense. A line like the second one—'cor malastruc, enfastijat de viure' [blundering heart, weary of life]—hardly seems possible in any other language: the clotted texture of the consonants conveys superbly the self-reproach of the beginning.[1] All this is of a piece with the terrifying allegory of life and death which comes in the second and third stanzas. One hardly needs to insist on the details, on the gestures like 'Braços oberts és eixida a carrera' [Death has come out into the street with open arms] and 'Ab ulls plorant e cara de terror' [With weeping eyes and face of terror], but it is worth noticing the paradox that binds these together. What happens, quite simply, is that the customary rôles of life and death are reversed: to the man who is tired of life, death is a consolation; it is the aspect of *life* that is terrifying: it cries out—and this is the final twist—as *death* cries to the fortunate man.

What follows is less intense, but only relatively so. Again, there is the idea that the poet has been singled out by love, that lesser lovers will fail to learn from him at their peril. And this leads up to one of Ausias March's characteristic formulae, the phrase with which he invariably asserts his personal identity: 'io són aquell…'—'I am the man whom one should pity'. But here, the formula which in other poems is stated with arrogance is undermined by the pathos of the situation:

the rest of the stanza has a dying fall, as one by one he lists the sources of vitality from which he is cut off. It is only in the last four lines that one is made to feel that this is a love poem at all: the hope is presumably the hope that the woman has denied him. If this is so, one may feel the reaction is excessive: the reader could hardly be blamed for passing over this reference to love. Yet what remains constant to the very end of the poem is the sense of alienation, of being dead to the world. Thinking back to the opening of the poem, we are made to realize that the speaker has even been denied what then seemed the consolation of death: his life is 'finished' only in a social sense (this is the real meaning of *civilment*) and his soul will have to live on, 'condemned in this world', and, one imagines, with the prospect of being condemned in the next world as well.

In considering Ausias March's attitude to death, one has to be careful not to be led astray by Romantic ideas about love and the death-wish. At the same time, it involves more than the conventional notion of 'dying of love' which is so common in fifteenth-century poetry. What is much more relevant is the idea that in loving one risks one's spiritual health—one's soul, in fact. It seems true to say that Ausias March is only intermittently concerned with damnation in a specifically Christian sense, and we shall see some evidence for this later on. What concerns him much more is the destructive power of love and the extreme difficulty of avoiding this. When he comes to theorize about love, it is quite clear that he adopts the scheme that runs through the whole courtly love tradition, that is to say, that there are three kinds of love: spiritual love, animal passion or lust, and *amor mixtus*, which shares in both. It is possible, of course, to play a good many variations on these three concepts, and courtly love poetry as a whole shows plenty of examples of this. Where Ausias March goes further than most poets of this tradition is in exploring the frontier between the body and the spirit. Or rather, he writes very often as if there were no frontier. If love is a torment, as it clearly is in many of his poems, this is not simply a matter of the opposing natures of body and spirit. The tension arises because these two things constantly act on one another: each tries to invade the other, so that the flesh tries to rise into the orbit of the spirit, whereas the spirit is always inclined to

lower itself and sink to the level of the flesh. Though he some-
times writes as if a compromise were possible—the kind of
compromise implied in *amor mixtus*—basically he believes
that this is bound to fail, that the balance is too precarious,
and that the body will always win. This, in fact, is one of his
more specific criticisms of the troubadours. In one of his more
theoretical poems (LXXXVII), he dismisses those poets who
have described this type of compromise: 'The troubadours
write of this desire, and, for this reason, mortal grief afflicts
them; their appetites feed on the senses'. In fact, he goes
further than this: not only can the body and the spirit never be
reconciled, but, he argues, there is a conflict within the spirit
itself. Just as the body and the spirit tend to usurp one
another's domains, so the spirit is torn apart when love
degenerates into the selfish passion of the instincts.

This is the central source of tension in Ausias March; how-
ever much he tries to argue himself out of it—and he does
this at times with great subtlety—it is something to which he
is always forced to return. And even when he uses more con-
ventional terms—when he is writing, for instance, quite
simply about 'dying of love'—these are always liable to
throw up some of his most memorable images. From the
poem already discussed, it should be clear that death is a
subject that tends to engage the full power of his imagination.
One theme that comes over very strongly in some of his other
poems is his sense of companionship with the dead, the reverse
side of the isolation he feels among the living. So one poem—
XIII—begins:

> Colguen les gents ab alegria festes
> lloant a Déu, entremesclant deports;
> places, carrers e delitables horts
> sien cercats ab recont de grans gestes;
> e vaja io los sepulcres cercant,
> interrogant ànimes infernades,
> e respondran, car no són companyades
> d'altre que mi en son continu plant.
> [Let people celebrate feast days and be glad, praising
> God (and) playing games between times; let squares,
> streets and pleasant gardens be filled with tales of great
> deeds; and let me walk among tombs, questioning the
> souls of the damned; and they will reply, for they have no

one but me to accompany them in their continual lament.]
Or, more pathetic still, the vision of dead lovers which opens
LXXIX:

> Oh vós, mesquins, qui sots terra jaeu
> del colp d'Amor ab lo cos sangonent,
> e tots aquells qui ab lo cor molt ardent
> han bé amat, prec-vos no us oblideu!
> Veniu plorant, ab cabells escampats,
> oberts los pits per mostrar vostre cor
> com fón plagat ab la sageta d'or
> ab què Amor plaga els enamorats.

> [O you, wretched ones, who lie underground, your
> bodies bleeding from the stroke of Love, and all those
> who, with burning hearts, have loved well, I pray you,
> do not forget! Come weeping, with dishevelled hair,
> your breasts open to show how your hearts were pierced
> by the arrow of gold with which Love wounds those (who
> are) in love.]

These are the kinds of image which stayed in the minds of
certain Spanish poets of the sixteenth and seventeenth cen-
turies who attempted to translate or to imitate Ausias March.
Yet, powerful as these images are, they are not followed up in
the poems in which they occur. If we read on in the last
poem, we find ourselves plunged into a description of the
arrows of Love, based on a passage from an earlier troubadour
poet, Guiraut de Calansó. And in the previous poem, the
transition is if anything more abrupt; the very next line reads:
'Cascú requer e vol a son semblant' [Everyone seeks and
desires his like]—a commonplace statement which ultimately
derives from Aristotle. This last example brings us to a very
striking feature of Ausias March, which so far I have only
touched on in passing: his tendency to indulge in large-scale
philosophical argument. This in itself is nothing new: there is
a good deal of philosophizing in some of the later troubadours,
like Guiraut Riquier and Sordello, and various critics have
seen in this the influence of contemporary scholasticism.
Where Ausias March differs is in the lengths to which he is
prepared to go, and in his fairly exact knowledge of scholastic
theory. It would, in fact, be possible to piece together most
of the basic principles of medieval philosophy from his poems.
This has encouraged certain critics to speak of him as a

philosophical poet, as a writer with a basically intellectual cast of mind. This seems an exaggeration: certainly, it is surprising to find such detailed knowledge in a Valencian nobleman of the fifteenth century, though it hardly goes beyond what we would expect to find in any reasonably educated scholar of the time. It is clear, for instance, that Ausias March was familiar with certain passages in the *Ethics* of Aristotle, and that he must have read a certain amount of Aquinas, if not in the original text, at least in some kind of compendium. To take one example, it is noticeable that when he speaks of virtue, he bases himself on the Thomist distinction between natural and divine virtues, and when he refers to this double nature of man, he coins the term *el compost* ('the compound'), which corresponds to Aquinas's use of *compositus* and *conjunctus*.

None of this, of course, tells us anything about the quality of the poetry. What we *can* say is that, at the very least, it provides Ausias March with a consistent frame of reference within which to analyse his feelings. In his less successful poems, he does this and little else, and the result can be monotonous. And even in some of his better poems, as we have seen, there are disconcerting shifts from concrete, personal passages to abstract, moralizing ones. In his finest work, however, the combination often succeeds magnificently, just because, through the use of allegory and simile, he is able to present his abstractions in concrete terms. So, in one poem (x), he describes a king who rules over three cities: after years of indecisive struggle with his enemy, the latter defeats him by employing the services of a mercenary. After his defeat, the king is deprived of one of the cities, but is allowed to govern the other two as a vassal. In the later part of the poem, the allegory is worked out: the three cities are the three powers of the soul—memory, understanding and will; the enemy is Love, who has defeated the speaker through the power of a single body, that of the woman to whom the poem is addressed; the lost city corresponds to his memory of the past; his understanding and will, on the other hand, are now the woman's lieutenants...and so on. The allegory is worked out exactly, with no sense of strain, and the result is a poem that re-creates the conventional abstractions in terms of a vivid corner of the feudal world.

The essential point here is not that Ausias March should have tried to present a consistent doctrine of love in the abstract—which he doesn't, however hard certain scholars have worked to provide one—but that he should have used these principles, whenever they seemed relevant, to gloss and analyse his personal experience of love. In his best poems, the experience always comes first, so that we receive the full power of the impact before we are invited to try and understand it. What is unique in Ausias March, then, is his ability to combine the two things: there must have been many sinful lovers at the time—some of them poets—who knew no theology, and many theologians who, whatever their experience of love, never put it into verse, still less into verse with a scholastic flavour.

On the one hand, therefore, his poetry is continually testing personal experience by submitting it to rational analysis. On the other, it is a kind of poetry that often tries to extend that experience, to make it more universal, by comparing it with other human situations. Here, Ausias March's mind tends to work by analogy: time after time he begins a poem by saying 'I am like the man who...', or 'Like one who... so it is with me'. And it is in this type of poem that we are made most aware of the kind of images that seem to have haunted his imagination. These, almost without exception, are sombre and disturbing: comparisons drawn from the sick-bed, the prison cell and the dangers of the elements, particularly the sea. And if he uses the imagery of war, as he often does, it is not of victorious feats of arms that he thinks, but of the man whose courage fails him as he goes into battle. A poem like the one that begins: 'Així com cell qui en lo somni es delita...' (1) [Like the man who takes pleasure in dreams...] depends to a great extent on such comparisons. The basic theme here, of course, is the same that Dante puts into the mouth of Francesca da Rimini at one of the most moving moments in the *Divine Comedy*: 'Nessun maggior dolore/che ricordarsi del tempo felice/nella miseria...'. The various comparisons that Ausias March uses to amplify the thought do not need any comment: though one can find literary precedents for one or two of them, the way he links them together is very personal and utterly characteristic. And certainly, it is these that carry the weight of the poem, rather than the last four lines, which, as sometimes happens with his *envois*, stand rather apart from the rest, like tiny epigrams which condense the most intimate part of his personal experience.

His sea images, as I have suggested, strike the same note as the others, even in poems where the personal situation is not especially violent. The sea, for Ausias March, is perhaps the greatest of all symbols of turbulence, as in this splendid stanza from XLVI:

> Bullirà el mar com la cassola en forn,
> mudant color e l'estat natural,
> e mostrarà voler tota res mal
> que sobre si atur un punt al jorn;
> grans e pocs peixs a recors correran
> e cercaran amagatalls secrets:
> fugint al mar, on són nodrits e fets,
> per gran remei en terra eixiran.
> [The sea will boil like a pot in the oven, changing its colour and natural state, and it will appear to hate anything which rests on it for a moment; fish great and small will rush to save themselves and will search for secret hiding-places: escaping from the sea where they were born and bred, they will leap on to dry land as a last resort.]

What strikes one in all these images is the reluctance to idealize: the only criterion, one feels, is not an aesthetic one, but quite simply whether the image helps to illuminate the experience. With this in mind, we can turn to the remarkable sequence of six poems usually known as the *Cants de mort*. There is no doubt that they form a single cycle, that they all refer to the death of the same woman, and that this woman is quite distinct from the woman addressed in other cycles. All the poems are beautifully sustained, but the most striking of all is the fifth. It is here that the concern to know the fate of the dead woman comes to a climax. The poet's grief stems from the fact that he does not know whether, as he puts it, 'God has taken her to himself', or whether He has 'buried her in Hell', and, because of this uncertainty, he does not know how to address her. If her soul is saved, he goes on, there is no need to pray for her, but if she is in Hell, a terrible thought arises when he reflects that he may himself have been the cause of her damnation:

> Si és així, anul.la'm l'esperit,

> sia tornat mon ésser en no-res,
> e majorment si en lloc tal per mi és;
> no sia io de tant adolorit.
>
> [If it is the latter, cancel my spirit, let my being return to
> nothingness, the more so if she is in such a place because
> of me; let me not suffer such anguish.]

This is perhaps the most terrible problem of conscience in the
whole of his work: the idea that he may have brought about
another person's damnation. And the poem ends with an
appeal to the woman to return as a ghost to relieve his un-
certainty:

> Tu, esperit, si res no te'n defèn,
> romp lo costum que dels morts és comú;
> torna en lo món e mostra què és de tu:
> lo teu esguard no em donarà spavent.
>
> [You, spirit, if nothing prevents you from it, break the
> custom which is common to the dead; come back to
> earth and show what has become of you: your look will
> not cause me terror.]

To whom could these poems possibly be addressed? In the
case of Ausias March's other poems, it would hardly help us
to know; *those* women, we can safely say, fall entirely within
the terms of the courtly love tradition. But there are several
passages in the *Cants de mort* that should make us pause. In
the middle of the third poem, for instance, there is a stanza
that appears to be addressed to the general reader:

> Molts són al món que mos dits no entengueren
> e ja molts més que d'aquells no sentiren.
> ¿ Qui creure pot que entre amors vicioses
> voler honest treball per estar simple,
> gitant de si maravellós efecte
> estant secret per força dels contraris?
> Dolç i agre ensems, llur sabor no és distinta;
> ella vivint, mos volers aitals foren.
>
> [There are many on earth who have not understood my
> writings, and many more who have never heard of them.
> Who can believe that, among shameful loves, an honest
> desire should struggle to be alone, pouring forth the
> marvellous effect which had been hidden by the power of
> contraries? Sweet and bitter at once, their flavour is not
> separate; while she was alive, such were my desires.]

Though the expression is a little enigmatic in places, what he appears to be saying is that those who know what he has previously written about sinful passion may fail to recognize that he is now talking about an honest love. In this same poem, he goes on to refer to his relations with the woman when she was still alive. There is no sense here of an un-attainable love; the references are all to particular places and moments which they shared in their experience, and which are still there to remind the poet of her now that she is dead. Not only this, in two of the other poems there are references to her actual death:

> Tot quant Amor e Por me pogren noure,
> finí lo jorn que li viu los ulls cloure. (xcii)
> [All injuries that Love or Fear could do me came to an end on the day when I saw her close her eyes.]

And, even more strikingly:

> Quan l'esperit del cors li viu partir
> e li doní lo darrer besar fred (xcv)
> [When I saw her spirit part from her body and I gave her a last cold kiss.]

And, most memorable of all, in the final poem of the series:

> Enquer està que vida no finí,
> com prop la mort io la viu acostar,
> dient plorant:—No vullau mi lleixar,
> hajau dolor de la dolor de mi!—
> [(Her) life had still not come to an end when I saw her draw near to death, saying with tears: 'Please do not leave me, have pity on my suffering!']

What does all this mean? Quite simply, I think, that we can hardly imagine this situation as one that involves another man's wife. Try to imagine these poems as referring to 'Llir entre cards' or 'Plena de seny' and the differences stand out immediately. These are surely—and one cannot doubt the sincerity of the poems—a woman's last words, addressed to the man she loves, who is beside her death-bed. And there are two final passages that we should take into account, both from the first poem in the series. One contains a striking epitaph:

> e lo meu cos, ans que la vida fine,
> sobre lo seu abraçat vull que jaga.
> Ferí'ls Amor de no curable plaga;
> separà'ls Mort: dret és que ella els veïne.

Lo jorn del Juí, quan pendrem carn e ossos,
mescladament partirem nostres cossos.

[and, before my life ends, I wish my body to lie with its
arms around hers. Love dealt them an incurable wound;
Death separated them; it is right that she should bring
them together. On the Day of Judgement, when we take
on flesh and bone, we shall share out our bodies without
distinction.]

The other is briefer:

Als que la Mort toll la muller aimia
sabran jutjar part de la dolor mia.

[Those from whom Death has taken away the woman they
loved will be able to judge part of my suffering.]

The crucial phrase is *muller aimia: aimia* is a standard word in
courtly love poetry meaning 'loved one', 'beloved'; *muller*
means 'woman', but also 'wife'. 'Loved woman'? 'Beloved
wife'? One cannot be sure, but in view of all the other
passages just quoted, one is tempted to say the latter. And,
bearing in mind the lines that contain the epitaph, one cannot
fail to be struck by a sentence from the poet's will: 'I wish
and command that the body or bones of the honourable lady
Johana Scorna, my former wife (i.e. his second wife) be
transferred, if permission be granted…from the town of
Gandia, where she was buried, to the aforesaid sepulchre of
the March family in the Cathedral of Valencia, where I
myself wish to be buried'. All this is no more than a hypo-
thesis, but if it were true—and at least it seems plausible—it
would mean that here, in some of the most moving poetry he
ever wrote, Ausias March has left behind the courtly tradition
in a quite unprecedented way.

Taken as a whole, the *Cants de mort* are poems that attempt
to deal with the possibilities of salvation and damnation, that
is to say, with matters that lie at the centre of Christian belief.
In these particular poems, Ausias March does not try to
generalize about such questions; whenever he considers them
it is always in the context of the relationship between himself
and the dead woman, a relationship that, as we have seen,
continues to exist after death. We might be tempted to think
that he had no need to generalize, that he completely accepted
the Thomist interpretation of Christianity, parts of which find
their way into the more speculative passages of his verse. Yet

this would not be entirely true: belief, after all, is more than just a matter of intellectual assent, and it would be surprising if Ausias March, who questions so much in his own experience, were not equally introspective about his relation to Christianity. Here again, his attitude seems to fluctuate a good deal in the course of his work. For example, in some of his more conventional poems, where he is writing fairly close to the orthodox courtly love tradition, he accepts that his love is sinful and blasphemous but suggests that he simply does not care. This on the whole, though, is rather rare, just as, at the other end of the scale, it is rare for him to write a whole poem in praise of Christ. However, there is one poem, the so-called *Cant espiritual* (CV), in which he seems to speak with unusual directness, and where he sums up a great deal of what we find scattered through the rest of his work.

In general terms, it seems fair to say that, whenever Ausias March refers to God, it is nearly always as a judge, and one whose justice may often seem like cruelty. This is certainly true of the *Cants de mort*, where he is lamenting the death of a particular woman whose loss he finds hard to bear. And it is also true, though the context is quite different, of the *Cant espiritual*. The whole poem, which runs to over two hundred lines, is cast in the form of a prayer, and the general sense is quite clear: the poet wishes to achieve salvation, but feels that he is too weak to do so without the help of God. Of all the poems of Ausias March, this is the one that goes furthest along the line of self-reproach, and it does this with remarkable honesty. This is not just a question of confessing to various sins; it is also a recognition of the poet's failure in his relations with God. At one point he says 'Io tem a Tu més que no et só amable' [I fear, rather than love, you], and this inability to feel genuine love for God is at the heart of the poem and its tensions. For one thing, he is caught between his fear of death and the wish to die before he commits any more sins, and for another, he recognizes that there can be no possible salvation without love. And so he says, at the climax of the poem:

Dóna'm esforç que prenga de mi venja.
Io em trob ofès contra Tu ab gran colpa,
e si no hi bast, Tu de ma carn te farta,
ab què no em tocs l'esperit, que a Tu sembla;

> e sobretot ma fe que no vacil.le
> e no tremol la mia esperança;
> no em fallirà caritat, elles fermes,
> e de la carn, si et suplic, no me n'oges.
>
> [Give me the strength to take vengeance upon myself. I find I have offended you with great sin; and if I am too weak, gorge yourself on my flesh, but do not touch my spirit, which resembles you; and, above all, may my faith not wander nor my hope tremble; charity will not fail me if they are firm, and if I pray to you for my flesh, do not listen to me.]

The poem does not quite end here, but, as one would expect, what follows offers no easy solution. One critic, Joan Fuster, has said that God, for Ausias March, is no more than the basic piece in a moral system, at most a judge, but in no sense the active, personal God of Christianity.[2] One sees what he means, though he is surely oversimplifying. What is clear, here and elsewhere, is Ausias March's total inability to delude himself, to appear to believe what, in fact, he cannot. Because of the energy of his verse and the intensity of his self-inquiry, the results are never merely negative. And, though there are many things in his verse which are unmistakably medieval, this is why he can at times seem almost modern.

Apart from his Catalan imitators, two separate generations of Spanish poets, one in the 1530s and 40s and another in the early seventeenth century, treated him practically as a contemporary. In the course of this period, he was translated several times into Spanish and once into Latin.[3] And, even in English, there are times when one seems to catch his characteristic note. Here, for instance, are some verses by an English poet who is known to have travelled in Spain and to have possessed books in Spanish:

> Thou art like a pilgrim, which abroad hath done
> Treason, and durst not turn to whence he is fled,
> Or like a thief, which till death's doom be read,
> Wisheth himself deliverèd from prison;
> But damned and haled to execution,
> Wisheth that still he might be imprisonèd...

Or, remembering Ausias March's poem about the king who owned three cities:

I, like an usurp'd town, to another due,
Labour to admit You, but Oh, to no end!
Reason, Your viceroy in me, me should defend,
But is captiv'd, and proves weak or untrue...

The poet, of course, is John Donne, and both passages come from the *Holy Sonnets*. Coincidence? Possibly: but at least they show a persisting habit of mind, and a similar tendency to reach for a particular kind of simile in moments of intense introspection. Both Donne and Ausias March, one might say, are poets who submit their undisciplined lives to the discipline of verse, and in doing so create memorable poems. And one phrase of Ausias March stays in the mind as a superb expression of the state from which so much of his poetry derives: 'en tot lleig fet hagué lo cor salvatge' (LXVIII) [in every base action, his was a savage heart], an appropriate note on which to leave a poet whose sheer intelligence and energy enabled him to use the existing tradition to produce great poetry.

THE TEXT. The spelling of the Catalan text has been modernized, except where this would involve a change of pronunciation. This seems legitimate, and even essential, in an anthology that is intended for non-specialists, and those who require a more scholarly text may refer to the edition by Pere Bohigas listed in the Bibliography. It should also be noted that many editions follow the manuscript tradition of indicating the caesura after the fourth syllable—a constant feature of the decasyllabic line as used by Ausias March and earlier poets—by means of a space. Thus, in Bohigas's edition, the first stanza of I appears as follows:

Axí com cell   qui.n lo somni .s delita
e son delit   de foll pensament ve,
ne pren a mi,   que.l temps passat me té
l'imaginar,   qu. altre bé no.y habita,
sentint estar   en aguayt ma dolor,
sabent de cert   qu.en ses mans he de jaure.
Temps de .venir   en negun bé .m pot caure;
aquell passat   en mi és lo millor.

VERSIFICATION. As the orthography of the Bohigas text emphasizes, the correct scansion of such verse depends on a number of contracted forms (qui.n = qui + en, que.l = que + el, qu.altre = que + altre, etc.) which in modern

Catalan can be represented simply by the slurring of adjacent vowels. Certain other combinations that involve the suppression of a consonant (e.g. co.l= com+ el) have been retained, since there is no way of reproducing them in modern Catalan.

The great majority of Ausias March's poems are composed in eight-line stanzas, rhyming *abbacddc*. Occasionally, as in XCII, this stanza form is extended by the addition of a rhyming couplet: *abbacddcee*. A small number of poems, including the *Cant espiritual* (CV), are written in unrhymed stanzas or *estramps*. In all these forms, the basic metrical unit is the decasyllable, with its final stress on the tenth syllable. As previously indicated, this line divides into two hemistichs of unequal length, with a caesura after the fourth syllable—a fact that contributes greatly to the distinctive rhythms of March's verse.

PRONUNCIATION. Though this is not the place for a complete study of Catalan pronunciation,[4] a few points should be noted for the benefit of readers unfamiliar with the language:

1) Unlike Spanish, Catalan relaxes its unstressed vowels, as in *casa* [kázə], *terra* [térrə], *orella* [uréʎə]. (Unstressed *i* between two vowel sounds resembles the consonant *y* in English *yes*: *feien* [féjən]; unstressed *u* between two vowels is like the consonant *w* in English *away*: *creuen* [kréwən].)

2) *c* is soft before *e* or *i* and hard in most other positions. *ç* is used as in French.

ig usually sounds like English *tch*: *lleig* [ʎetʃ], *desig* [dəzítʃ]. At the end of a word and when not preceded by accented *i*, it is unvoiced: *càstig* [kástik].

j is like *s* in English *measure*: *joc* [ʒɔ́k], *jardí* [ʒərðí].

ll is a palatal, like *lli* in English *William*: *filla* [fíʎə]. When separated by a dot, the two *l*s are pronounced independently: *intel.ligent* [intəlliʒén].

ny Spanish *ñ* or the *ni* in English *onion*.

p is silent after *m* when in the same syllable: *temps* [téms].

qu before *e* or *i* = English *k*; before *a* or *o*, it is like *qu* in English *quota*.

Final *r* is often, though not always, silent. It is never pronounced at the end of infinitives: *saber* [səßé], *dormir* [durmí].

s between vowels or before a voiced consonant is voiced: *casa* [kázə]; an unvoiced *s* between vowels is represented by *ss*: *massa* [másə].

Final *t* after *l* or *n* is silent: *molt* [mól], *dormint* [durmín].

x at the beginning of a word or after a consonant = English *sh*; it has the same sound when preceded by a vowel + *i*: *això* [əʃɔ́], *mateix* [mətéʃ].

z is like *z* in English *zero*.

3) Catalan has the following range of diphthongs: *ai, ei, oi, ui, au, eu, iu, ou, uu*. In each case, the first vowel has its normal value and the second is a semi-consonant [j] or [w]. To these one should add *ua, üe, üi, uo* after *g* or *q*, where the *u* is a semi-consonant [w].

4) Catalan uses two written accents, the acute (´) and the grave (`), which, as well as indicating stress, denote a closed or an open vowel respectively.

5) The basic stress rules are as follows:

The stress falls on the penultimate syllable of words ending in (i) a vowel but not a diphthong; (ii) a vowel (excluding diphthongs) + *s*; *-en* or *-in*.

The stress falls on the final syllable of words ending in (i) a diphthong or a diphthong + *s*; (ii) any group of consonants; *n* after *a, o* or *u*; any other single consonant except *s*.

A phonetic transcription of the first stanza of I in present-day 'standard' Catalan would run as follows:

əʃí kɔ́m séʎ kín lu sɔ́mniz ðəlítə
Així com cell qui en lo somni es delita

é son dəlíd də foʎ pənsəmém bé
e son delit de foll pensament ve,

nə prɛ́n ə mí kəl téms pəsád mə té
ne pren a mi, que el temps passat em té

liməʒiná káltrə βé nój əβítə
l'imaginar, que altre bé no hi habita.

səntín əstán əɣwájd ma ðuló
Sentint estar en aguait ma dolor

saβén də sɛrt kən səz mánz é ðə ʒáwrə
sabent de cert que en ses mans he de jaure,

témz ðəβəní ən nəɣúm bém pɔ́t káwrə
temps d'avenir en negun bé em pot caure;

əkéʎ pəsát əm mí éz lu miʎó
aquell passat en mi es lo millor.

At this distance in time, it is impossible to know with complete accuracy how March's poems must have sounded when they were originally composed. It is worth bearing in mind, however, that Valencian pronunciation—of which there are frequent signs in the poems—differs in certain ways from 'standard' Catalan:

1) Stressed *e* and *o* are more open than in Catalan.

2) Unstressed vowels retain their full value, as in Spanish.

3) Final *r* and final *t* after a consonant are normally pronounced.

4) *x* (initial or after a consonant) = *ch*, as in English *church*.

5) Voiced sibilants (i.e. *-s-*, *tz̧*, *j*, *tj*) tend to become unvoiced: *casa* [kása], *dotz̧e* [dótse], *juny* [tʃuɲ], *pitjor* [pitʃor].[5]

THE TRANSLATIONS. In providing literal prose translations, my chief aim has been to enable the reader who knows another Romance language (not necessarily Spanish) to follow the meaning, and especially the syntax, of the original poems. The term 'literal translation' itself is, of course, a very relative one, since degrees of 'literalness' may vary considerably, and it is at least arguable whether verse can ever be 'translated' in any serious sense as prose. In this instance, I have tried to keep as close as possible to the structure and word-order of the originals, even when this has meant a certain awkwardness in the English. March's grammar is often loose or elliptical by modern standards, and the peculiar energy of his verse often depends on this fact. It would have been easy to gloss over such effects in translation; instead, wherever some kind of expansion seemed necessary in English, I have usually indicated this by the use of parentheses. I need hardly add that my versions have no literary pretensions whatsoever; their only purpose is to bring the non-Catalan reader a little closer to the work of a major poet who deserves to be seen in a wider European context.

Finally, I should like to thank all those who have helped, knowingly or otherwise, in the preparation of this anthology, and especially Dr Alan Yates, who read the manuscript and made a number of valuable comments. I am also indebted to Ernest Benn Ltd. for permission to use certain passages from my *Catalan Literature* (London 1972).

NOTES

1. Most commentators have remarked on the particularly harsh texture of March's verse, which comes over very sharply when it is read aloud. March himself often draws attention to this: apart from his general claim that he writes 'without art', he admits at one point (LXXII) that his verses 'do not flatter the reader's ear' [l'orella d'hom afalac no pot rebre]. Far from being a defect, this seems part of a conscious attempt to adapt and extend troubadour practice by achieving a greater sincerity of tone.

2. Ausias March, *Antologia poètica,* ed. Joan Fuster (Barcelona 1959) 35.

3. The principal early translations are as follows: (into Spanish) Baltasar de Romaní (1539), Jorge de Montemayor (1560); (into Latin) Vicenç Mariner (1634). See also M. de Riquer, *Traducciones castellanas de A. M. en la Edad de Oro* (Barcelona 1946).

4. For a much fuller treatment of Catalan pronunciation, see the excellent volume on Catalan by Dr Alan Yates in the 'Teach Yourself' series (Hodder and Stoughton, London 1975) 1–25, and also the chapter on pronunciation by M. W. Wheeler in the 4th edition of Joan Gili's *Catalan Grammar* (Dolphin Book Co. Ltd., Oxford 1974) 11–23.

5. At the time of writing, a recording of seven poems of Ausias March, read by J. Palau Fabre, is available from *Discos Vergara*. The settings recorded for *Discophon* by the well-known Valencian singer Raimon are also highly recommended.

The Poems

I

Així com cell qui en lo somni es delita
e son delit de foll pensament ve,
ne pren a mi, que el temps passat me té
l'imaginar, que altre bé no hi habita.
Sentint estar en aguait ma dolor,
sabent de cert que en ses mans he de jaure,
temps d'avenir en negun bé em pot caure;
aquell passat en mi és lo millor.

Del temps present no em trobe amador,
mas del passat, que és no-res e finit;   10
d'aquest pensar me sojorn e em delit,
mas quan lo perd, s'esforça ma dolor
sí com aquell qui és jutjat a mort
e de llong temps la sap e s'aconhorta,
e creure el fan que li serà estorta
e el fan morir sens un punt de record.

Plagués a Déu que mon pensar fos mort,
e que passàs ma vida en dorment!
Malament viu qui té lo pensament
per enemic, fent-li d'enuigs report;   20
e com lo vol d'algun plaer servir
li'n pren així com dona ab son infant,
que si verí li demana plorant
ha tan poc seny que no el sap contradir.

Fóra millor ma dolor soferir
que no mesclar poca part de plaer
entre aquells mals, qui em giten de saber
com del passat plaer me cové eixir.
Las! Mon delit dolor se converteix;
doble és l'afany aprés d'un poc repòs,   30
si co.l malalt qui per un plasent mos
tot son menjar en dolor se nodreix;

com l'ermità, qui enyorament no el creix
d'aquells amics que tenia en lo món,
essent llong temps que en lo poblat no fón,   *over*

I

Like the man who takes pleasure in dreams and his pleasure
comes from foolish thoughts, so it happens to me, for time
past occupies my imagination and no other good dwells there.
Feeling my suffering to lie in wait, knowing for certain that I
must fall into its hands, time future cannot turn out well for
me; that past is the best (part) of me.

I am no lover of the present, but of the past, which is nothing
and (is) finished; I take comfort and pleasure in this thought,
but when I lose it, my suffering increases: like the man who is
condemned to death, and has known this for a long time and
takes courage, and they make him think he will be reprieved,
and put him to death without a moment for remembering
(his past).

I wish to God that my thoughts were dead and I could spend
my life in sleeping! He lives poorly who has his thought for
enemy, bringing him news of troubles; and when it tries to
provide him with some pleasure, he is like the woman with
her child, who, if it cries and begs her for poison, has so little
sense that she cannot refuse it.

It would be better to endure my suffering than to mix a tiny
part of pleasure with those evils which drive me out of my
mind when the time comes for me to leave behind former
pleasure. Alas! my pleasure turns to suffering; labour is
doubled after a little rest, like the sick man who, for one
pleasant mouthful, turns everything he eats into suffering;

like the hermit in whom there grows no longing for those
friends he had in the world, not having been for a long time
near habitation,

per fortuit cas un d'ells li apareix,
qui los passats plaers li renovella,
sí que el passat present li fa tornar;
mas com se'n part, l'és forçat congoixar:
lo bé, com fuig, ab grans crits mal apella.   40

Plena de seny, quan amor és molt vella,
absença és lo verme que la gasta,
si fermetat durament no contrasta,
e creurà poc, si l'envejós consella.

I I

Pren-me enaixí com al patró que en platja
té sa gran nau e pensa haver castell;
veent lo cel ésser molt clar e bell,
creu fermament d'una àncora assats haja.
E sent venir sobtós un temporal
de tempestat e temps incomportable;
lleva son jui: que si molt és durable,
cercar los ports més que aturar li val.

Moltes veus és que el vent és fortunal,
tant que no pot sortir sens lo contrari,   10
e cella clau qui us tanca dins l'armari
no pot obrir aquell mateix portal.
Així m'ha pres, trobant-me enamorat,
per sobres-alt qui em ve de vós, ma aimia:
del no amar desalt ne té la via,
mas un sol pas meu no hi serà trobat.

Menys que lo peix és en lo bosc trobat
e los lleons dins l'aigua han llur sojorn,
la mia amor per null temps pendrà torn,
sol coneixent que de mi us doneu grat;   20
e fiu de vós que em sabreu bé conèixer,
e, conegut, no em serà mal graïda
tota dolor havent per vós sentida;
lladoncs veureu les flames d'amor crèixer.   *over*

(and) by chance one of them appears and reminds him of his past pleasures, so that he makes the past present for him; but when the friend goes away, he is forced to grieve: when good departs, it summons evil with loud cries (to take its place).

Wise lady: when love is very old, absence is the worm that devours it, unless constancy struggles hard, and it mistrusts the advice of the envious.

II
I am like the master whose ship lies close to shore and he thinks it (as safe as) a castle; seeing that the sky is quite clear and fine, he firmly believes that with a single anchor he has enough. And he sees approaching a sudden spell of storm and impossible weather; he calculates that if it lasts for long, it would be better for him to seek harbour than to stay.

It often happens that the wind is capricious; so much so, that he cannot set sail without the contrary wind, and that key which shuts you in the cupboard cannot open the same door. So it has happened to me, being in love, through the boundless pleasure I receive from you, my beloved: displeasure is the way which leads to not-loving, but not a single step of mine will be found there.

Less than fish are found in woods and lions dwell in water will my love ever change, as long as I know that you take pleasure in me; and I am confident that you will come to know me well, and, once you have known me, all the suffering I have felt because of you will not go unrewarded; then you will see the flames of love increase.

Si mon voler he dat mal a parèixer,
creeu de cert que vera amor no em lluny:
pus que lo sol és cald al mes de juny,
ard mon cor flac sens algun grat merèixer.
Altre sens mi d'açò mereix la colpa;
vullau-li mal, com tan humil servent   30
vos té secret per son defalliment;
cert, és Amor que mi, amant, encolpa.

Ma volentat ab la raó s'envolpa
e fan acord, la qualitat seguint,
tals actes fent que el cos és defallint
en poc de temps una gran part de polpa.
Lo poc dormir magresa al cos m'acosta,
dobla'm l'enginy per contemplar Amor;
lo cos molt gras, trobant-se dormidor,
no pot dar pas en aquesta aspra costa.   40

Plena de seny, donau-me una crosta
del vostre pa, qui em lleve l'amargor;
de tot menjar m'ha pres gran dessabor,
si no d'aquell qui molta amor me costa.

III
Alt e amor, d'on gran desig s'engendra,
e esper, vinent per tots aquests graons,
me són delits, mas dòna'm passions
la por del mal, qui em fa magrir carn tendra;
e port al cor sens fum continu foc,
e la calor no em surt a part de fora.
Socorreu-me dins los térmens d'una hora,
car mos senyals demostren viure poc.

Metge escient no té lo cas per joc
com la calor no surt a part extrema;   10
l'ignorant veu que lo malalt no crema
e jutja'l sa, puis que mostra bon toc.
Lo pacient no porà dir son mal,
tot afeblit, ab llengua mal diserta;   *over*

If I have expressed my desire badly, be sure that it does not make true love (any more) distant from me; hotter than the sun in the month of June, my frail heart burns without receiving any favour. Another, not myself, is to blame for this; think badly of him, since he conceals from you such a humble servant as myself through his weakness; certainly, it is Love who accuses me, (now that I am) in love.

My will combines with my reason and they agree, pursuing quality, performing such actions that in a short time the body loses a good part of its flesh. Lack of sleep brings thinness to my body, my wit is doubled by thinking of love; the fat body which is given to sleeping cannot take a single step on this rocky shore.

Wise lady: give me a crust of your bread, to take away the bitterness from me; I have conceived a great distaste for all food, except that which costs me much love.

III

Pleasure and love, from which great desire is born, and hope, which passes through all these stages, are sources of delight to me, but the fear of misfortune, which makes my tender flesh grow thin, brings me suffering; and I carry in my heart a continual fire without smoke, and the heat does not reach my outer part. Help me within the space of an hour, for my symptoms show that I shall not live much longer.

A wise doctor does not take the case lightly when the heat does not come to the surface; the ignorant one sees that the sick man has no fever and thinks him well, since he is healthy to the touch. The patient cannot describe his illness, weak as he is, with clumsy tongue;

gests e color assats fan descoberta,
part de l'afany, que tant com lo dir val.

Plena de seny, dir-vos que us am no cal,
puis crec de cert que us ne teniu per certa;
si bé mostrau que us está molt coberta
cella per què Amor és desegual.   20

IV

Així com cell qui desija vianda
per apagar sa perillosa fam,
e veu dos poms de fruit en un bell ram,
e son desig egualment los demanda,
no el complirà fins part haja elegida,
sí que el desig vers l'un fruit se decant,
així m'ha pres dues dones amant,
mas elegesc per haver d'Amor vida.

Sí com la mar se plany greument e crida,
com dos forts vents la baten egualment,   10
u de llevant e l'altre de ponent,
e dura tant fins l'un vent ha jaquida
sa força gran per lo més poderós,
dos grans desigs han combatut ma pensa,
mas lo voler vers u seguir dispensa;
io el vos public: amar dretament vós.

E no cuideu que tan ignocent fos
que no veés vostre avantatge gran;
mon cos no cast estava congoixant
de perdre lloc qui l'era delitós.   20
Una raó fón ab ell de sa part,
dient que en ell se pren aquesta amor,
sentint lo mal o lo delit major,
sí que ell content, cascú pot ésser fart.

L'enteniment a parlar no venc tard,
e planament desféu esta raó,
dient que el cos, ab sa complexió,
ha tal amor com un llop o renard;

over

his gestures and colour are sufficient indications, apart from his agony, which speaks for itself.

Wise lady: I do not need to say I love you, since I firmly believe that you are sure of it; although you show that the reason why Love is unequal is well concealed in you.

IV

Like the man who desires food to satisfy his dangerous hunger and sees two clusters of fruit on a fine branch, whose desire covets them both equally, and who will not appease it until he has chosen one or the other: so it has happened to me in loving two women, but I choose so that Love may grant me life.

As the sea complains deeply and cries out when two strong winds attack it equally, one from the east, the other from the west, and (this) lasts until one of the winds abandons its great strength to the more powerful one, two great desires have assailed my thoughts, but my will decides to follow one of them; I proclaim my intention to you: to love you honestly.

And do not think I was so foolish as not to see your great superiority before this; my unchaste body was afraid to lose a place which gave it pleasure. The body had one argument for its part, saying that in it this love originates, and that it (is the body which) feels most pain or pleasure (from this), so that, if the body is content, each one may be satisfied.

The understanding was not slow to speak, and utterly refuted this argument, saying that the body, because of its composition, loves in the same way as a wolf or a fox;

que llur poder d'amar és limitat,
car no és pus que apetit brutal,   30
e si l'amant veeu dins la fornal,
no serà plant e molt menys defensat.

Ell és qui venç la sensualitat;
si bé no és en ell prim moviment,
en ell està de tot lo jutjament:
cert guiador és de la voluntat.
Qui és aquell qui en contra d'ell reny?
Que voluntat, per qui el fet s'executa,
l'atorg senyor, e si ab ell disputa,
a la perfí se guia per son seny.   40

Diu més avant al cos ab gran endeny:
"Vanament vols e vans són tos desigs,
car dins un punt tos delits són fastigs,
romans-ne llas, tots jorns ne prens enseny.
Ab tu mateix delit no pots haver:
tant est grosser que Amor no n'és servit;
volenterós acte de bé és dit,
e d'aquest bé tu no saps lo carrer.

Si bé complit lo món pot retener,
per mi és l'hom en tan sobiran bé,   50
e qui sens mi esperança el reté
és foll o pec e terrible grosser".
Aitant com és l'enteniment pus clar,
és gran delit lo que per ell se pren,
e son pillard és subtil pensament,
qui de fins pasts no el jaqueix endurar.

Plena de seny, no pot Déu a mi dar,
fora de vós, que descontent no camp;
tots mos desigs sobre vós los escamp;
tot és dins vós lo que em fa desijar.   60

for their power to love is limited, since it is no more than brute appetite, and if you see the lover (burn) in the fire, he will not be pitied, much less defended.

It is the understanding which conquers sensuality; even though the first impulse does not come from it, in it resides the judgement of all things: it is the sure guide of the will. Who is the man who strives against it? For the will, through which the deed is performed, acknowledges the understanding as master, and, though it may disagree with it, in the end is guided by its wisdom.

And it continues to address the body with great scorn: 'You wish vainly and your desires are vain, for in an instant your pleasures turn to loathing, and you are tired of them: every day you are made aware of this. You can take no pleasure in yourself: you are so gross that you do Love no service; Love is said to be a voluntary act of good, and you do not know the way to this good.

If the world can contain perfect good, through me man achieves this supreme good, and whoever hopes (to obtain it) without me is foolish or stupid and monstrously uncouth.' The clearer the understanding, the greater the pleasure which one receives through it, and its pillar is subtle thought, which does not allow it to fast from delicate foods.

Wise lady: apart from you, God cannot give me anything in which there is no dissatisfaction; I scatter all my desires on you: everything that makes me desire is within you.

X

Sí com un rei, senyor de tres ciutats,
qui tot son temps l'ha plagut guerrejar
ab l'enemic, qui d'ell no es pot vantar
mai lo vencés, menys d'ésser-ne sobrats,
ans si al matí l'enemic lo vencia,
ans del sol post pel rei era vençut,
fins que en les hosts contra el rei fón vengut
un soldader qui lo rei desconfia;

lladoncs lo rei perdé la senyoria
de les ciutats, sens nulla posseir,   10
mas l'enemic dues li'n volc jaquir,
dant fe lo rei que bon compte en retria
com a vassall, la renda despenent
a voluntat del desposseïdor;
de l'altra vol que no en sia senyor
ne sia vist que li vinga en esment:

llong temps Amor per enemic lo sent,
mas jamés fón que em donàs un mal jorn
que en poc instant no li fes pendre torn,
foragitant son aspre pensament;   20
tot m'ha vençut ab sol esforç d'un cos,
ne l'ha calgut mostrar sa potent força:
los tres poders que en l'arma són me força,
dos me'n jaqueix, de l'altre usar no gos.

E no cuideu que em sia plasent mos
aquest vedat, ans n'endure de grat;
si bé no puc remembrar lo passat,
molt és plasent la càrrega a mon dors.
Jamés vençó fón plaer del vençut
sinó de mi que em plau que Amor me vença   30
e em tinga pres ab sa invisible llença,
mas paren bé sos colps en mon escut.

De fet que fui a sa mercè vengut,
l'Enteniment per son conseller pres
e mon Voler per alguatzir lo mes,   *over*

X

Like a king, master of three cities, who all his life has been
pleased to make war on his enemy, who cannot boast that he
ever defeated him without being overcome in his turn, for, if
in the morning the enemy defeated him, by sunset he had been
beaten by the king, until in the armies opposed to the king
there came a mercenary who conquered him;

then the king lost his mastery over the three cities, (and was)
dispossessed of them all; but the enemy was willing to leave
him two, the king pledging himself to render good account of
them as a vassal, spending the income from them as the us-
urper should wish; as for the third city, the latter does not
wish the king to govern it or let it be seen that he has any
thought of it:

for a long time I have felt Love to be my enemy, but he has
never given me a bad day without my instantly making him
change, banishing from me his bitter thoughts. (Now) he has
totally defeated me with the strength of a single body; he has
had no need to display his mighty power: he overcomes the
three faculties of my soul; he leaves me two, (and) I dare not
use the other.

And do not think that what he has forbidden me is a pleasant
morsel; on the contrary, I willingly do without it; although I
cannot remember the past, its weight at my back is very agree-
able. Defeat was never a pleasure for the defeated except in
my case, for I am glad that Love should defeat me and keep
me prisoner in his invisible net: his strokes fall gratefully
upon my shield.

As soon as I fell into Love's hands, he took my Understanding
as his adviser and appointed my Will executor,

dant fe cascú que mai serà rebut
en sa mercè lo companyó Membrar,
servint cascú llealment son ofici,
sí que algú d'ells no serà tan nici
que en res contrast que sia de amar.   40

Plena de seny, vullau-vos acordar
com per Amor vénen grans sentiments,
e per Amor pot ser hom ignocents,
e mostre-ho io qui n'he perdut parlar.

XI

¿ Quins tan segurs consells vas encercant,
cor malastruc, enfastijat de viure,
amic de plor e desamic de riure ?
¿ Com soferràs los mals qui et són davant ?
Acuita't, doncs, a la mort qui t'espera.
E per tos mals te allongues los jorns:
aitant és lluny ton delitós sojorns
com vols fugir a la Mort falaguera.

Braços oberts és eixida a carrera,
plorant sos ulls per sobres de gran goig;   10
melodiós cantar de sa veu oig,
dient: 'Amic, ix de casa estrangera.
En delit prenc donar-te ma favor,
que per null temps home nat l'ha sentida,
car io defuig a tot home que em crida,
prenent aquell qui fuig de ma rigor'.

Ab ulls plorant e cara de terror,
cabells rompent ab grans udolaments,
la Vida em vol donar heretaments
e d'aquells dons vol que sia senyor,   20
cridant ab veu horrible i dolorosa,
tal com la Mort crida al benauirat
(car si l'hom és a mals aparellat,
la veu de Mort li és melodiosa).

over

each promising that their companion Memory would never be admitted to their grace, each one loyally performing his duty, so that neither would be so foolish as to oppose anything which had to do with loving.

Wise lady: please remember how from Love there comes great suffering and that through Love one may be reduced to childishness: I, who have lost the power of speech, am evidence of this.

XI

What certain guidance do you seek, (my) blundering heart, weary of life, a friend to tears and enemy to laughter? How will you bear the evils which lie before you? Hurry, then, towards the death which waits for you. Through your sufferings you prolong your days: the further off is your pleasant resting-place, the more you try to escape from comforting Death.

Death has come out into the street with open arms, her eyes weeping from excess of joy; I hear her voice sing melodiously, saying: 'Friend, leave this strange house. I take delight in granting you my favour, which no man born has ever experienced, for I avoid all those who call on me, taking the man who tries to escape my severity'.

With weeping eyes and face of terror, tearing her hair with great howls, Life tries to give me her inheritance and to make me master of these gifts, crying with dreadful, grieving voice, just as Death cries out to the fortunate man (for if a man is prepared for suffering, the voice of Death is melodious to him).

Bé em meravell com és tan ergullosa
la voluntat de cascun amador;
no demanant a mi qui és Amor,
en mi sabran sa força dolorosa.
Tots, maldient, sagramentejaran
que mai Amor los tendrà en son poder,   30
e si els recont l'acolorat plaer,
lo temps perdut, sospirant, maldiran.

Null hom conec o dona a mon semblant,
que, dolorit per Amor, faça plànyer;
io són aquell de qui es deu hom complànyer,
car de mon cor la sang se'n va llunyant.
Per gran tristor que li és acostada,
seca's tot jorn l'humit qui em sosté vida,
e la tristor contra mi és ardida,
e en mon socors mà no s'hi troba armada.   40

Llir entre cards, l'hora sent acostada
que civilment és ma vida finida;
puis que del tot ma esperança és fugida,
ma arma roman en aquest món damnada.

XIII
Colguen les gents ab alegria festes,
lloant a Déu, entremesclant deports;
places, carrers e delitables horts
sien cercats ab recont de grans gestes;
e vaja io los sepulcres cercant,
interrogant ànimes infernades,
e respondran, car no són companyades
d'altre que mi en son continu plant.

Cascú requer e vol a son semblant;
per ço no em plau la pràtica dels vius.   10
D'imaginar mon estat són esquius;
sí com d'hom mort, de mi prenen espant.   *over*

I wonder greatly that every lover's will should be so proud; without asking me who is Love, they will recognize in me his painful strength. All, cursing, will swear that Love will never hold them in his power, but if I describe to them the deceptive pleasure, they will sigh and curse the time they have lost.

I know no man or woman who is like me, who, wounded by Love, is to be pitied; I am the man whom one should pity, for my heart's blood is draining away. Because of the great grief which has come to it, the moisture which sustains my life is steadily drying up, and sadness has risen against me: not a single hand takes up arms to help me.

Lily among thorns: I feel the hour is approaching when my life among other men will end; since all my hope has flown, my soul remains condemned in this world.

XIII

Let people celebrate feast days and be glad, praising God (and) playing games between times; let squares, streets and pleasant gardens be filled with tales of great deeds; and let me walk among tombs, questioning the souls of the damned; and they will reply, for they have no one but me to accompany them in their continual lament.

Everyone seeks and desires his like; thus I take no pleasure in the company of the living. They are reluctant to imagine my condition; they are terrified of me, as of a dead man.

Lo rei xipré, presoner d'un heretge,
en mon esguard no és malauirat,
car ço que vull no serà mai finat,
de mon desig no em porà guarir metge.

Cell Teixion qui el buitre el menja el fetge
e per tots temps brota la carn de nou,
e en son menjar aquell ocell mai clou;
pus fort dolor d'aquesta em té lo setge,   20
car és un verm qui romp la mia pensa,
altre lo cor, qui mai cessen de rompre,
e llur treball no es porà enterrompre
sinó ab ço que d'haver se defensa.

E si la mort no em dugués tal ofensa
—fer mi absent d'una tal plasent vista—,
no li graesc que de terra no vista
lo meu cos nu, qui de plaer no pensa
de perdre pus que lo imaginar
los meus desigs no poder-se complir;   30
e si em cové mon darrer jorn finir,
seran donats térmens a ben amar.

E si en lo cel Déu me vol allojar,
part veure a Ell, per complir mon delit
serà mester que em sia dellai dit
que d'esta mort vos ha plagut plorar,
penedint vós com per poca mercè
mor l'ignocent e per amar-vos martre:
cell qui lo cos de l'arma vol departre,
si ferm cregués que us dolríeu de se.   40

Llir entre cards, vós sabeu e io sé
que es pot bé fer hom morir per amor;
creure de mi que só en tal dolor,
no fareu molt que hi doneu plena fe.

The King of Cyprus, imprisoned by a heretic, is not unfortunate, compared with me, since what I wish for will never be achieved: no doctor will cure me of my desire.

I am besieged by a suffering greater than that of Tityos, whose liver is devoured by a vulture, and each time the flesh is renewed, though the bird never ceases to feed on it: for one worm gnaws my thoughts, another my heart, and neither rests, and their work can only be interrupted by that which is forbidden to me.

And (even) if death did not inflict such a penalty—to deprive me of so pleasant a sight—I should not thank it for not clothing in earth my naked body, which expects to lose no other pleasure than that of imagining that my desires will never be achieved; and if I must end my last day, there will also be an end to good loving.

And if God wishes me to dwell in Heaven, apart from seeing Him, for my pleasure to be complete, it will be necessary for them to tell me there that it has pleased you to shed tears at my death, repenting that, because of your meagre favours, there dies an innocent man and a martyr to loving you: he who would (gladly) separate body from soul, if he could really believe that you would pity him.

Lily among thorns: we both know that a man may well die of love; the least you can do is believe with all your heart that my suffering is as great as I say.

XVIII

Fantasiant, Amor a mi descobre
los grans secrets que als pus subtils amaga,
e mon jorn clar als hòmens és nit fosca,
e visc de ço que persones no tasten.
Tant en Amor l'esperit meu contempla,
que par del tot fora del cos s'aparte,
car mos desigs no són trobats en home,
sinó en tal que la carn punt no el torba.

Ma carn no sent aquell desig sensible,
e l'esperit obres d'amor cobeja;   10
d'aquell cec foc qui els amadors s'escalfen,
paor no em trob que io me'n pogués ardre.
Un altre esguard lo meu voler pratica
quan en amar vós, dona, se contenta,
que no han cells qui amadors se mostren
passionats e contra Amor no dignes.

Si fos Amor substança raonable
e que es trobàs de senyoria ceptre,
béns guardonant e punint los demèrits,
entre els mellors sols me trobara fènix;   20
car io tot sols desempare la mescla
de lleigs desigs qui ab los bons s'embolquen;
càstic no em cal, puis de assaig no em tempten;
la causa llur és en mi feta nulla.

Sí com los sants, sentints la llum divina,
la llum del món conegueren per ficta,
e menyspreants la glòria mundana
puis major part de glória sentien,
tot enaixí tinc en menyspreu e fàstic
aquells desigs qui, complits, Amor minva,   30
prenint aquells que de l'esperit mouen,
qui no és lassat, ans tot jorn muntiplica.

Sí com sant Pau Déu li sostragué l'arma
del cos perquè vés divinals misteris,
car és lo cos de l'esperit lo carçre
e tant com viu ab ell és en tenebres,   *over*

XVIII

In my imaginings, Love reveals to me the great secrets which it hides from the most subtle, and my clear day is dark night to men, and I live by that which ordinary people do not taste. My spirit contemplates Love to such an extent that it seems to separate itself completely from the body, for my desires are not to be found in any man, except in him who is not troubled at all by the flesh.

My flesh does not feel that desire of the senses, and my spirit covets works of love; I have no fear of burning in that blind fire in which lovers grow hot. When my will finds happiness in loving you, my lady, its gaze is quite different from the gaze of those who show themselves to be sensual lovers, unworthy of Love.

If Love were a rational substance and held the sceptre of majesty, rewarding good and punishing faults, he would find me to be the one phoenix among the best; for I alone renounce the horde of base desires which mingle with the good; there is no need to punish me, since they do not try to tempt me; their cause is a dead letter as far as I am concerned.

Just as the saints, seeing the divine light, realized that the light of the world was false, despising earthly glory because they experienced a greater one, so I feel scorn and loathing for those desires which, (once they are) satisfied, cause Love to diminish, choosing those which arise from the spirit, which never tires, but multiplies continually.

As God removed the soul of Saint Paul from his body so that he might see divine mysteries (for the body is the soul's prison and as long as the soul dwells in it, it is in darkness),

així Amor l'esperit meu arrapa
e no hi acull la maculada pensa,
e per ço sent lo delit que no es cansa,
sí que ma carn la vera amor no em torba.   40

Pren-me enaixí com aquell filosofe
qui, per muntar al bé qui no es pot perdre,
los perdedors llançà en mar profunda,
creent aquells l'enteniment torbassen.
Io, per muntar al delit perdurable,
tant quant ha el món gros plaer de mi llance,
creent de cert que el gran delit me torba
aquell plaer que en fàstic, volant, passa.

Als naturals no par que fer-se pusquen
molts dels secrets que la deitat s'estoja,   50
que revelats són estats a molts martres,
no tan subtils com los ignorants i aptes.
Així primors Amor a mi revela,
tals que els sabents no basten a compendre,
e quan ho dic, de mos dits me desmenten,
dant aparer que folles coses parle.

Llir entre cards, lo meu voler se tempra
en ço que null amador sap lo tempre;
ço fai Amor, a qui plau que io senta
sos grans tresors; sols a mi els manifesta.   60

XIX

Oïu, oïu, tots los qui bé amats,
e planyeu mi si deig ésser plangut,
e puis veeu si és tal cas vengut
en los presents ne en los qui són passats!
Doleu-vos, doncs, de mi, vostre semblant
en soferir la dolor delitable,
car tost de mi se dolrà lo diable
com veurà mi semblant mal d'ell passant.

over

so Love carries off my spirit and does not take with it any impure thoughts, and thus I experience the pleasure which never grows tired, so that my flesh does not disturb true love.

I am like the philosopher who, in order to rise to the good that cannot perish, cast his perishable goods into the deep sea, thinking they would hinder his understanding. I, in order to rise to lasting good, throw away all the gross pleasures of the world, firmly believing that my supreme joy would be troubled by that pleasure which quickly turns to loathing.

Human beings feel that many of the secrets which God keeps in store are unattainable, though these have been revealed to many martyrs (who are) not as clever as the scholars who have no knowledge of such things. So Love reveals subtleties to me, which the learned do not succeed in mastering, and, when I speak, they deny my words, giving to understand that I am talking nonsense.

Lily among thorns: my will is tempered in that whose temper no lover knows; this is the work of Love, who wishes me to see his great treasures; he reveals them only to me.

XIX

Oyez, oyez, all you who love truly, and pity me if I deserve to be pitied, and then see if there has been such a case in the present age or in times past! Pity me, then, your fellow-man, who suffers this pleasant pain, for soon the devil himself will pity me when he sees me going through torment like his own.

¿ Qui és l'hom viu, tal dolor sofertant,
que desig ço de què se desespera ?   10
Aitant és greu que no par cosa vera
desijar ço de què és desesperant.
No só enganat de mon mal estament:
tot quant pratic tornar me sent en dan;
menys de poder me trob, havent-lo gran,
car no m'esforç per mostrar mon talent.

Mon primer mal és mon esperdiment,
per què m'aïr e per no res m'acús;
e lo segon és terrible refús
que vós mostrau si us feia enqueriment.   20
Portat me trob a molt prop de ma fi,
puis mon voler cas impossible guarda;
no tardarà l'hora, que ja fos tarda,
que tendré els peus en l'avorrit camí.

Si per null temps en contra Amor fallí,
io en són reprès, planyent-me'n l'enemic,
e mai vers mi poguí ésser amic,
car per null temps poder hi despenguí.
Hoc lo voler me trob en abundança,
mas del poder no en sé pus empobrit,   30
car io peresc e són tan defallit
que no puc dir: 'En vós és ma esperança'.

Una sabor d'agre e dolç Amor llança
que lo meu gust departir-les no sap:
dins mos delits dolor mortal hi cap,
e tal dolor ab delit ha lligança.
Mas io em reprenc com parlar m'ha plagut
de ço que en mi no basta la ciència;
sobres-amor me porta ignocència:
vull e desvull sens cas esdevingut.   40

Llir entre cards, creeu l'amador mut
i al canviant de punt en punt color,
e al pauruc com se membra d'Amor;
de l'atrevit sia son temps perdut.

What man alive, enduring such pain, desires what he despairs of? It is so severe that it seems incredible that anyone should wish for that of which he has no hope. I have no illusions about my unfavourable condition: I feel that everything I perform turns out to my disadvantage; though my strength is great, I find myself lacking in strength, since I make no attempt to reveal my inclination.

My first misfortune is my corrupt nature, because of which I get angry and accuse myself for no reason; and the second is the terrible refusal you give me if I court you. I find myself brought very close to my end, since my desire has an impossible aim; the hour will not delay, for it is already late, when I shall set foot on the hateful road.

If at any time I sinned against Love, I have been punished (for it), (so that even) my enemy has pitied me for it, and I have never been able to be a friend to myself, for I have never made the effort. Certainly, I have will to spare, but I know of no one who is so weak in strength, for I am dying and am so feeble that I cannot say: 'In you is my hope!'

Love has a bittersweet flavour which my taste is unable to separate: my pleasures contain mortal suffering and such suffering is bound up with pleasure. But I reproach myself for having allowed myself to speak of what my knowledge does not reach to; excess of love makes me like a child: I desire and do not desire for no reason.

Lily among thorns: believe the lover who is dumb and him who changes colour from one moment to the next, and the timid man when he thinks of Love; as for the bold lover, may his time be wasted.

XXIII

Lleixant a part l'estil dels trobadors
qui, per escalf, traspassen veritat,
e sostraent mon voler afectat
perquè no em torb, diré el que trob en vós.
Tot mon parlar als qui no us hauran vista
res no valdrà, car fe no hi donaran,
e los veents que dins vós no veuran,
en creure a mi, llur arma serà trista.

L'ull de l'hom pec no ha tan fosca vista
que vostre cos no jutge per gentil;   10
no el coneix tal com lo qui és subtil:
hoc la color, mas no sap de la llista.
Quant és del cos, menys de participar
ab l'esperit, coneix bé lo grosser:
vostra color i el tall pot bé saber,
mas ja del gest no porà bé parlar.

Tots som grossers en poder explicar
ço que mereix un bell cos e honest;
jóvens gentils, bons sabents, l'han request,
e, famejants, los cové endurar.   20
Lo vostre seny fa ço que altre no basta,
que sap regir la molta subtilea;
en fer tot bé s'adorm en vós perea;
verge no sou perquè Déu ne volc casta.

Sol per a vós basta la bona pasta
que Déu retenc per fer singulars dones:
fetes n'ha assats molt sàvies e bones,
mas compliment Dona Teresa el tasta;
havent en si tan gran coneixement
que res no el fall que tota no es conega;   30
a l'hom devot sa bellesa encega;
past d'entenents és son enteniment.

Venecians no han lo regiment
tan pacific com vostre seny regeix
subtilitats (que l'entendre us nodreix)
e del cos bell sens colpa el moviment.   *over*

XXIII

Leaving aside the manner of the troubadours, who, carried away by passion, exceed the truth, and restraining my own amorous desire so that it does not distract me, I shall say what I find in you. All my speech will be in vain to those who have not seen you, for they will not believe it; and those who see you, if they cannot see within, will be sad at heart when they believe me.

The eye of the ignorant man is not so dim that he will not fail to recognize the grace of your body; he does not know it as the subtle man does: the colour, yes, but he knows nothing of the texture. Whatever belongs to the body but does not share in the spirit, the coarse man knows well. He may be familiar with your colour and bearing, but he will not be able to speak properly of your gesture.

We are all coarse when we try to express what a fair and honest body deserves; well-bred young men, who are expert (in such matters), have pursued it, but, though (they are) hungry, are obliged to go on suffering (hunger). Your intelligence does what no other is capable of, for it can command great subtlety: in performing all good things, indolence sleeps in you; you are no virgin, since God wished you to bear offspring.

The good substance which God kept in order to make notable women sufficed for you alone; He has made a fair number (who are) very wise and good, but it is my Lady Teresa who tastes of perfection; possessing in herself such great knowledge that she lacks nothing to make herself wholly known: her beauty blinds the devout man; her understanding is food for those who understand.

The government of the Venetians is not as well-ordered as (the way in which) your intelligence rules over subtleties—which are nourished for you by understanding—and over the flawless movement of your lovely body.

Tan gran delit tot hom entenent ha
e ocupat se troba en vós entendre,
que lo desig del cos no es pot estendre
a lleig voler, ans com a mort està.   40

Llir entre cards, lo meu poder no fa
tant que pogués fer corona invisible;
meriu-la vós, car la qui és visible
no es deu posar lla on miracle està.

XXIX

Si com lo taur se'n va fuit pel desert
quan és sobrat per son semblant qui el força,
ne torna mai fins ha cobrada força
per destruir aquell qui l'ha desert,
tot enaixí em cové llunyar de vós,
car vostre gest mon esforç ha confús;
no tornaré fins del tot haja fus
la gran paor qui em tol ser delitós.

XXXIX

Qui no és trist, de mos dictats no cur,
o en algun temps que sia trist estat;
e lo qui és de mals passionat,
per fer-se trist no cerque lloc escur:
llija mos dits mostrants pensa torbada,
sens alguna art, eixits d'hom fora seny;
e la raó que en tal dolor m'empeny
Amor ho sap, qui n'és causa estada.

Alguna part, e molta, és trobada
de gran delit en la pensa del trist,   10
e si les gents ab gran dolor m'han vist,
de gran delit ma arma fón companyada.
Quan simplement Amor en mi habita,
tal delit sent que no em cuid ser al món,
e com sos fets vull veure de pregon
mescladament ab dolor me delita.   *over*

All who understand (these things) feel great delight and make it their occupation to understand you, since desire for the body cannot extend to base impulses: rather is it as though (it were) dead.

Lily among thorns: my power is not so great that it could make for you an invisible crown. You deserve one, since a visible crown should not be placed where there is a miracle.

XXIX

Like the bull who goes off into the wilderness when he is beaten by another of his kind who is too strong for him, and does not come back until he has recovered his strength to destroy the one who has injured him, so I must go away from you, for your action has weakened my courage; I shall not return until I have completely driven out the great fear which prevents me from being happy.

XXXIX

Anyone who is not sad or has not at some time been sad should pay no attention to my works; and he who suffers misfortunes should not look for a dark place in which to be sad: let him read my writings, which reveal troubled thoughts, uttered without art by one who is out of his mind; and Love, who has caused it, knows the reason which drives me to such suffering.

One part—and a great one—of supreme pleasure is found in the thoughts of the sad man, and if people have seen in me great suffering, my soul was accompanied by great joy. When Love dwells in me indivisibly, I feel such pleasure that I forget that I am in this world, and when I try to see his deeds from within, he gives me pleasure mixed with suffering.

Prest és lo temps que faré vida ermita
per mils poder d'Amor les festes colre;
d'est viure estrany algú no es vulla dolre,
car per sa cort Amor me vol e em cita.   20
E io qui l'am per si tan solament,
no denegant lo do que pot donar,
a sa tristor me plau abandonar
e per tostemps viuré entristadament.

Traure no pusc de mon enteniment
que sia cert e molt pus bell partit
sa tristor gran que tot altre delit,
puis hi recau delitós llanguiment.
Alguna part de mon gran delit és
aquella que tot home trist aporta,   30
que, planyent si, lo plànyer lo conforta
més que si d'ell tot lo món se dolgués.

Ésser me cuid per moltes gents reprès
puis que tant llou viure en la vida trista,
mas io qui he sa glòria a l'ull vista,
desig sos mals puis delit hi és promès.
No es pot saber, menys de l'experiença,
lo gran delit que és en lo sols voler
d'aquell qui és amador verdader
e ama si veent-se en tal volença.   40

Llir entre cards, Déu vos dón coneixença
com só per vós a tot extrem posat;
ab mon poder Amor m'ha enderrocat
sens aquell seu d'infinida potença.

The time is near when I shall live like a hermit, the better to keep Love's feast days; no one should pity me for this strange way of life, for Love wants me for his court and sends for me. And I, who love him for his own sake, not refusing the reward he may give, willingly abandon myself to his sadness and shall live sadly for ever.

I cannot get out of my mind that Love's great sadness may be a certain and much nobler fate than any other pleasure, since pleasant languor is involved in it. One part of my great pleasure is that which any sad man is allowed, for, when such a person laments his situation, his complaining comforts him more than if the whole world pitied him.

I think I shall be reproached by many people for praising so highly the life of sadness, but I who have seen its glory with my own eyes desire its evils, since they promise pleasure. One cannot know, except by experience, the great pleasure which exists in the mere intention of him who is a true lover and loves himself for being of such a mind.

Lily among thorns: may God make you realize how for your sake I have exposed myself to every extreme; Love has demolished me with my own strength, not with his own, of infinite power.

XLVI

Veles e vents han mos desigs complir,
faent camins dubtosos per la mar.
Mestre i Ponent contra d'ells veig armar;
Xaloc, Llevant, los deuen subvenir
ab llurs amics lo Grec e lo Migjorn,
fent humils precs al vent Tramuntanal
que en son bufar los sia parcial
e que tots cinc complesquen mon retorn.

Bullirà el mar com la cassola en forn,
mudant color e l'estat natural,   10
e mostrarà voler tota res mal
que sobre si atur un punt al jorn;
grans e pocs peixs a recors correran
e cercaran amagatalls secrets:
fugint al mar, on són nodrits e fets,
per gran remei en terra eixiran.

Los pelegrins tots ensems votaran
e prometran molts dons de cera fets;
la gran paor traurà al llum los secrets
que al confés descoberts no seran.   20
En lo perill no em caureu de l'esment,
ans votaré al Déu qui ens ha lligats,
de no minvar mes fermes voluntats
e que tots temps me sereu de present.

Io tem la mort per no ser-vos absent,
perquè Amor per mort és anul.lats;
mas io no creu que mon voler sobrats
pusca esser per tal departiment.
Io só gelós de vostre escàs voler,
que, io morint, no meta en mi oblit;   30
sol est pensar me tol del món delit
—car nós vivint, no creu se pusca fer—:

aprés ma mort, d'amar perdau poder,
e sia tost en ira convertit,
e, io forçat d'aquest món ser eixit,
tot lo meu mal serà vós no veer.   *over*

XLVI

Sails and winds will accomplish my desires, making dangerous paths across the sea. I see the mistral and the west wind take up arms against them; but the east and south-west winds will help them, with their friends the north-east and the south, humbly begging the tramontana to blow favourably on them, that all five may bring about my return.

The sea will boil like a pot in the oven, changing its colour and natural state, and it will appear to hate anything which rests on it for a moment; fish great and small will rush to save themselves and will search for secret hiding-places: escaping from the sea where they were born and bred, they will leap on to dry land as a last resort.

All pilgrims together will make vows and will promise many votive offerings of wax; the great fear will bring to light the secrets which will never be revealed to the confessor. In (such) danger, you will never leave my mind; rather shall I vow to the God who has bound us together not to lessen my firm intentions and to keep you continually present (to me).

I fear death because I do not want to leave you, for Love is cancelled by death; but I do not believe that my will can be overcome by such separation. I am afraid that your own faint will, if I should die, may cast me into oblivion; this thought alone takes away all pleasure on earth for me—for as long as we are alive, I do not believe this can happen—:

(that) after my death, you may lose your power to love and it may quickly be turned into anger, and (that), if I am forced to leave this world, my whole misfortune will be in not seeing you.

Oh Déu !, ¿ per què terme no hi ha en amor,
car prop d'aquell io em trobara tot sol ?
Vostre voler sabera quant me vol,
tement, fiant de tot l'avenidor.   40

Io són aquell pus extrem amador,
aprés d'aquell a qui Déu vida tol:
puis io són viu, mon cor no mostra dol
tant com la mort per sa extrema dolor.
A bé o mal d'amor io só dispost,
mas per mon fat Fortuna cas no em porta;
tot esvetlat, ab desbarrada porta,
me trobarà faent humil respost.

Io desig ço que em porà ser gran cost,
i aquest esper de molts mals m'aconhorta;   50
a mi no plau ma vida ser estorta
d'un cas molt fér, qual prec Déu sia tost.
Lladoncs les gents no els calrà donar fe
al que Amor fora mi obrarà;
lo seu poder en acte es mostrarà
e los meus dits ab los fets provaré.

Amor, de vós io en sent més que no en sé,
de què la part pijor me'n romandrà;
e de vós sap lo qui sens vós està.
A joc de daus vos acompararé.   60

LIV
¿ Qui, sinó foll, demana si m'enyor,
essent absent, d'aquella qui em fa viure ?
E si no plor, ¿ qui és lo qui em veu riure,
si bé no pas contínua dolor ?
Tots mos delits en u he transportat;
Amor li plau en mi fer aquest canvi;
lo món no té res valent lo recanvi
de l'esperant lo bé tan desijat.   *over*

O God! why is there no limit to love, that I might have come to it alone? I would have known how much your will desired me, fearing (and) trusting everything to the future.

I am that most extreme of lovers, after him whose life God takes away: since I am alive, my heart does not show such grief as in death, whose suffering is extreme. I am prepared for (the) good or (the) evil of love, but it is my fate that Fortune brings me no occasion (for either); wide awake, with door unbarred, it will find me humbly answering.

I desire what may cost me dear, and this hope consoles me for many evils; I do not wish my life to be exempted from a most grave event, which I pray God may come soon. Then people will not need to have faith in what Love performs outside me; its power will be shown in action and I shall prove my words by my deeds.

Love: I feel you (intuitively) rather than know you (by reason), so that the worse part will remain to me; he knows of you who is without you. I shall compare you to a game of dice.

LIV

Who but a fool asks me if, when I am absent, I miss that woman who makes me live? And if I do not weep, who sees me laugh, though I do not suffer continual pain? I have combined all my pleasures in one; it pleases Love to make this change in me; there is nothing in the world (which is) the equivalent of hoping for such a desirable good.

Tant és lo bé qui m'és davant posat,
que sens dolor visc aquell esperant;   10
si no l'atenc, seré tan malanant
que en aquest món infern hauré trobat.
Contentament la una part me dóna,
per l'altra és ma vida tribulada:
ab mort està en balança posada,
tement que por ma esperança confona.

De punt en punt ma esperança em bandona,
e venç-me por d'aquell mal que io em tem.
¿ Qui és aquell en poc amar extrem
que segurtat prenga per companyona?   20
Per molt amar en altre mi transport,
sí que esser pens tot la persona aquella;
seria el món una gran meravella
que no hagués por de la mala sort.

Viure en delit porta ab si por de mort,
car d'aquell és enemic sobirà,
e si Amor delit jamés portà
io só aquell qui en puc fer lo report.
Oh Mort, qui est de tots béns envejosa,
i en tal voler te segueix la Fortuna!   30
Cascuna prec que mudeu llei alguna,
no ressemblant a la qui m'és damnosa.

Saber-se pot ma vida perillosa
caent en mans d'enemics tan mortals;
pobres e rics senten sos aspres mals,
e cascú d'ells ab manera ergullosa.
Seguesquen mi tots los que amaran,
mon ris o plor qualque d'ells me seguesca,
car io són prest de tastar fel o bresca
per los qui mal o bé d'Amor pendran.   40

Llir entre cards, passions d'Amor fan
Tembre i Fiar estar dins un hostal;
de gran remor dubtar un punt no cal,
e guai d'aquells que entre llurs mans estan!

So great is the good which is set before me that I live in hope of it without suffering; if I do not achieve it, I shall be so wretched that I shall have found Hell in this world. On the one hand, it gives me great happiness; on the other, my life is full of trials; it is placed in the scales with death, afraid that fear will frustrate my hope.

More and more does hope abandon me, and the fear of that evil which I dread overwhelms me. What man is so unaccustomed to love that he will take certainty for a companion? Through much loving I become a different person, so much so, that I think I *am* that person; the world would be a great marvel if I were not afraid of misfortune.

To live in pleasure brings with it fear of death, for that is pleasure's chief enemy, and if Love ever brought pleasure, I am the man who can bear witness to it. O Death, who are envious of all good things, and in such purpose are assisted by Fortune! I implore you both to change your law, and not to resemble that (law) which is harmful to me.

One may know my life to be in danger, falling into the hands of such mortal enemies; both rich and poor feel their harsh evils, and each of them with (his) proud ways. Let all who are in love follow me, let some of them follow me in laughter, some in tears, for I am ready to taste gall or honey on behalf of those who will receive good or evil from Love.

Lily among thorns: Love's torments make Fear and Trust share the same lodgings; there is not the slightest doubt that there will be a great upheaval: and woe to those who are in their hands!

LXIII

¿ Qui em tornarà lo temps de ma dolor
e em furtarà la mia llibertat ?
Catiu me trob, llicenciat d'Amor,
e, d'ell partit, tot delit m'és llunyat.
Sí co.l senyor avorreix lo servent,
que null castic ne càrrec li vol dar,
així Amor me da bandonament,
que son poder en mi no el plau mostrar.

En ira està de Déu lo pecador
com en est món treball no li és dat;   10
dels béns de Déu no sia esperador:
no ha lloguer qui no ha treballat.
Així, d'Amor qui no sent lo turment,
en sos delits no es cure delitar;
tot amador prenga en açò esment:
que sens tristor no es pot molt alegrar.

Dolor és gran de tot fin amador,
com desesper li és davant posat;
mas, per mercè, Amor l'és donador
que d'esperar delit no és llançat;   20
goig e tristor li estan de present,
esper e por lluny li volen mostrar
son mal o bé, dels quals u tostemps sent,
e lo que perd aprés torna cobrar.

Aprés lo mal, qui sent de bé sabor
no pot ser dit del tot malauirat;
lo past d'amor no ha tanta amargor
que sus tot dolç no sia estimat.
De tal sabor no em conec sentiment,
e pus amarg que fel he de gustar,   30
car io sofir dolor d'enyorament
ne veig camí per algun bé esperar.

Qui d'Amor fuig, d'ell és encontrador,
e io qui el cerc dins mi, no l'he trobat;
en llocs lo veig difamat per traidor,
e fuig de mi qui l'he més que altre honrat.   *over*

LXIII

Who will give me back the time of my suffering and take away my liberty? I find myself a prisoner, (now that I am) set free by Love, and, having left him, all pleasure has gone from me. Just as the master detests his servant (so much) that he will give him neither punishment nor duties (to perform), so Love has cast me off, for he does not wish to demonstrate his power on me.

The sinner suffers God's anger when in this world he is sent no trials; let him not hope for God's benefits: he who has not laboured receives no pay. Thus, whoever does not feel Love's torment need not expect to enjoy his delights; every lover should bear this in mind: that, without sadness, there can be no great joy.

Every true lover suffers greatly when he is faced with despair; but, mercifully, Love allows him not to be deprived of the hope of pleasure; joy and sadness are present to him, hope and fear show him from a distance their good or evil, of which he always feels one or the other, and whichever he loses he later recovers.

After misfortune, anyone who experiences the taste of good cannot be said to be altogether unlucky; the food of love is not so bitter that it may not be considered sweeter than anything else. I have not experienced such a flavour, and I have to taste what is more bitter than gall, for I suffer the pain of longing and see no way of hoping for any good.

Whoever runs away from Love, finds him, and I, who search for Love within myself, have not found him; in some places I see him denounced as a traitor, and he avoids me, who have honoured him more than anyone.

Io no el deman dona en lo món vivent,
mas que dins mi ell vulla reposar;
sembla la mort, que encalça lo fugent
e fuig d'aquell qui la vol encontrar.   40

Cremat vull ser d'Amor per sa calor,
car dins son foc io em trobe refrescat,
si com lo sant, havent en Déu ardor,
en son turment se troba consolat.
Tant quant Amor és fort i en mi potent,
lo seu delit prop mi sent acostar;
si el trob escàs, altre m'ha fer content,
fora de mi mon delit he trobar.

Aitant pot fer d'Amor sa gran favor,
que bastarà fer que l'enamorat   50
no el tocarà esperança ne por:
tant estarà en goig present trobat!
Io em só oblidat havent tal sentiment;
propi és a mi tal estat desijar;
a l'ignorant desig no el ve en esment,
enemic és de Amor ignorar.

L'home no pot ser al món vividor,
si de humor mal serà netejat;
lo bo i el mal conserven la calor
d'hom radical, que sens ells és gastat.   60
Així d'Amor, qui lo seu mal no sent,
no pot en ell sa passió durar:
desig lo té, qui és de bé falliment,
i el bé atès, tal desig ha cessar.

Amor, Amor, io só ver penident
com de ingrat vos he volgut reptar
per no trobar lloc a mi convinent;
és lo defalt com io no pusc amar.

I do not ask him for any woman who lives on earth, merely that he should agree to dwell in me; he is like death, who catches the fugitive and flees from him who wishes to find her.

I want to be burned by Love's heat, for I find myself refreshed in his fire, just as the saint (who is) burning in God finds comfort in his torment. The stronger and more powerful Love is in me, the nearer to me I feel his pleasure come; if I find him ungenerous, another must make me content (and) I must find my pleasure outside myself.

Love's great favour is so powerful that it will be sufficient to preserve the lover from both hope and fear; in such present joy will he be found! I have forgotten that I (ever) had such a feeling; it is my nature to desire such a state; (this) desire never occurs to the ignorant: ignorance is the enemy of Love.

Man could not live in the world if it were cleansed of evil humours; good and evil preserve man's radical heat, without which he would be destroyed. Thus, if a man does not feel the pains of love, his passion cannot last: desire possesses him, which is a lack of good, and, (once) that good (is) achieved, such desire must fail.

O Love, o Love: I am truly sorry that I have accused you of ingratitude for not having found a place to suit me; this is the fault because of which I cannot love.

LXVI

Algú no pot haver en si poder
altre amar contra sa voluntat,
ne en ser tan fort, ab tanta potestat,
a deslligar los nuus que Amor sap fer.
Qui és lo foll qui em repte si no am?
Qui és lo foll reptant-me de amar?
Tal passió negú la pot forçar;
per què d'algú, si bé no em vol, no em clam.

Oh vera Amor!, tu invoc e reclam:
puis m'has plagat, vulles m'abandonar   10
aquell engüent que sol medicinar
los pacients que per tu mal passam.
No sia sols io en ta desfavor!
Ta pietat, mans juntes la requir;
no em dóns mercè, mas guardó del servir;
tant am quant pot hom fer amar Amor.

Oh tu, qui est sobirana dolor,
quan deseguals los volers fas unir!
No et veja tal, o m'atorga morir;
dolça em serà de la mort l'amargor.   20
Mostra'm la llum de vera esperança,
no pas aital com de tu vana em ve,
mas que raó la consenta prop sé.
No em vulles dar enganosa fiança!

Si co.l malalt de viure té fermança
per alguns mals que familiars té,
si algun mal d'altre accident li ve,
en por de mort l'imaginar lo llança,
ne pren a mé, que m'era ja no res
lo mal d'Amor, vivint sobre aquell,   30
e per mal nou, a morir vinc per ell,
per no ser tal e com molt major és.

Oh tu, Amor, a qui Déu ha permès
que de infant usar fas l'home vell,
e lo sabent d'ignocent no s'apell
puis que de tu ell no sia defès!

over

LXVI

No one can have it in his power to love another against his will, nor be so strong, with sufficient force to undo the knots which Love can tie. What fool will accuse me if I do not love? What fool will accuse me if I *do* love? No one can force such a passion: therefore I do not complain if anyone does not wish me well.

O true Love! I invoke and implore you: since you have wounded me, please grant me that ointment which cures us sufferers who are ill because of you. Let me not be the only one in your disfavour! With hands joined (in prayer), I beg your pity; grant me no favour, but reward for my service; I love as much as Love can make anyone love.

O you, who are supreme suffering when you join together unequal wills! Let me not see you thus, or let me die; death's bitterness will be sweet to me. Show me the light of true hope, not that vain hope which I receive from you, but that which reason consents to have near it. Do not give me deceitful confidence!

Just as the sick man clings to life because his ailments are familiar to him, if by chance some other kind attacks him, his imagination plunges him into mortal fear: so it is with me, for Love's sickness was nothing to me, (since I had been) living with it, and with a fresh ailment I come to die, since it is not like the other and is (much) greater.

O you, Love, whom God has allowed to make the old man act like a child, and (because of whom) the wise man may not consider himself blameless as long as he is not protected from you!

Tu est aquell aire molt pestilent
portant al món una plaga mortal;
ésser menys d'ulls, ans del colp, molt hi val,
mas al ferit mort sola és guariment.   40

Amor, Amor, lo jorn que l'Ignocent
per bé de tots fón posat en lo pal,
vós me ferís, car io em guardava mal,
pensant que el jorn me fóra defenent.

LXVIII

No em pren així com al petit vailet
qui va cercant senyor qui festa el faça,
tenint-lo cald en lo temps de la glaça
e fresc, d'estiu, com la calor se met;
preant molt poc la valor del senyor
e concebent desalt de sa manera,
veent molt clar que té mala carrera
de canviar son estat en major.

¿ Com se farà que visca sens dolor
tenint perdut lo bé que posseïa ?   10
Clar e molt bé no veu, si no ha follia,
que mai porà tenir estat millor.
Doncs, ¿ què farà, puix altre bé no el resta,
sinó plorar lo bé del temps perdut ?
Veent molt clar per si ser decebut,
mai trobarà qui el faça millor festa.

Io són aquell qui en lo temps de tempesta,
quan les més gents festegen prop los focs
e pusc haver ab ells los propris jocs,
vaig sobre neu, descalç, ab nua testa,   20
servint senyor qui jamés fón vassall
ne el venc esment de fer mai homenatge,
en tot lleig fet hagué lo cor salvatge,
solament diu que bon guardó no em fall.   *over*

You are that pestilential air that brings a mortal plague into the world; it would be better to have no eyes before receiving such a blow, but to him who is wounded, death alone is a cure.

O Love, o Love: on the day when the Innocent One for the good of all men was placed upon the Cross, you wounded me, for I defended myself badly, thinking the day itself would protect me.

LXVIII

I am not like the little page who seeks a master who will treat him well, keeping him warm in time of frost and cool in summer when the heat comes; despising the worth of his former master and taking a dislike to his behaviour, (but) realizing clearly that he has chosen a bad road in changing his situation for a higher one.

How will he manage to live without suffering, having lost the good which he possessed? He sees well and truly, unless he is a fool, that he will never find a better situation. Then what will he do, since no other good remains to him, except mourn the goodness of the time now lost? Seeing clearly that he has deceived himself, he will never find anyone to treat him better.

I am that man who, in time of storm, when most people enjoy themselves around the fire and I can join in their games, walk over snow, with naked feet, bareheaded, serving a master who was never a vassal nor ever thought to pay homage (to another); in every base action, his was a savage heart; he only tells me I shall not lack a good reward.

Plena de seny, lleigs desigs de mi tall;
herbes no es fan males en mon ribatge;
sia entès com dins en mon coratge
los pensaments no em devallen avall.

LXXIII

No pens algú que m'allarg en paraules
e que mos fets ab los dits enferesca,
ans prec a Déu que de present peresca,
si mon parlar atany en res a faules.
Mos fets d'amor ab los romans acorden,
que foren més que los escrits no posen;
cells qui d'amor en lo mal se reposen,
en creure mi, consciences no els morden.

Sens amor són aquells que ab mi discorden
e la dolor de amor temoregen,   10
e quan hi són, eixir d'ella cobegen
e per tots temps de si mateixs recorden.
Poc és amant qui dolor lo turmenta,
sí que volgués menyscabar de aquella;
dins la dolor és una meravella
que no sé com lo delit s'hi presenta.

Dolor d'amor a mi tant no turmenta
que eixir volgués de son amargós terme,
e si davant me veig d'absença verme
e lo conhort contra amor dant empenta,   20
io em dolc en tant de guarir de la plaga
que cerc verins per què lo conhort muira,
i en gran delit mon cor jamés abuira
fins que en amor ma pensa està vaga.

Un gran delit als amadors s'amaga,
a tots aquells que en molta amor no vénen:
en llur voler delit d'amor no prenen,
no senten bé, si esper no els falaga.   *over*

Wise lady: I cut off base desires from myself; no weeds grow on my riverbank; let it be understood that, deep in my heart, my thoughts do not drag me down.

LXXIII

Let no one think that I spin out my words, and that I exaggerate my deeds by my utterances: rather I pray God that I may die this instant if my speech ever borders on fiction. My deeds of love are like the Romans' (deeds), which were greater than the written accounts tell; those who dwell in love's sickness, in believing me, feel no remorse in their consciences.

Those who disagree with me are without love and fear love's suffering, and when they are in suffering, they long to leave it behind, and always think of themselves. The man who, tormented by such suffering, would have it reduced, is a poor lover; in suffering, it is a miracle that pleasure—I do not know how—should be present.

Love's suffering does not torture me to such an extent that I should wish to leave its bitter limits, and if I see before me the worm of absence, and (see) comfort struggling against love, I suffer so much in recovering from the wound that I search for poisons so that comfort may die, and my heart is never so full of pleasure as when my thoughts wander in love.

A great pleasure is hidden from lovers, from all those who do not achieve great love: in their desire, they do not take pleasure in love, nor do they experience good, if hope does not flatter them.

No és al món tan gran delit de pensa
com lo pensar en la persona amada,   30
e qui l'ateny, tota causa ha oblidada,
sí que a si no troba mentre hi pensa.

Tèbeu voler delit d'amor defensa;
els extrems han de bé complit semblança.
Lo poc voler no ha por ne esperança,
rebre no pot gran bé ne molta ofensa;
e l'alt extrem ell si mateix delita:
no recordant, del bé venint espera.
Cascú d'aquests ha la sua carrera,
e lo del mig no sap on se habita.   40

Io só aquell servent qui no despita
si no ateny del servei coneixença:
tot és aquell on ha sa benvolença
i en son voler tot lo seu habilita.
Tant en amor ma pensa en alt grau munta
que ma arma és dins en lo cos que ama,
e só content de qualsevulla fama:
en res de mi voluntat he defunta.

Dins si mateix veu gran glòria junta
qui de amor bé ne mal no espera,   50
altre amant ab voluntat sancera,
per ses virtuts, sens passió conjunta.
Nostre esperit sols béns e virtuts guarda
quan solament usa de sa natura,
amant per si aquella creatura
que les virtuts als vicis li són guarda.

Llir entre cards, qui d'amor se pren guarda,
tres parts se'n fan, dues seguint natura:
la una mor, e l'altra tostemps dura,
la terça és que fals apetit guarda.   60

There is in (all) the world no greater pleasure of the mind than to think of the person one loves, and whoever attains to this forgets everything else, so that he loses all sense of himself in thinking of her.

A lukewarm desire hinders the pleasure of love; extremes have the appearance of perfect good. The faint desire has neither fear nor hope, it cannot receive great good or much injury; and the high extreme (of love) is its own pleasure: remembering nothing, it hopes for future good. Each of these desires takes its own course, and no one knows where the medium lies.

I am that servant who bears no grudge if his service goes un-recognized: he exists solely where his goodwill lies and he places his entire will in hers. My thoughts rise to such a high degree in love that my soul is within the body which it loves, and I am content with any kind of reputation: in any concern of my own, my will is dead.

He who expects neither good nor evil from love sees a great glory gathered within himself, loving another with sincere intention, for her virtues, unmixed with sensual desire. Our spirit considers only good things and virtues when it acts entirely in accordance with its own nature, loving for her own sake that creature whose virtues protect her from vices.

Lily among thorns: whoever considers love (finds that) it has three parts, two of which follow nature: one dies and the other lasts for ever, the third is that which looks to false appetite.

LXXVII

No pot mostrar lo món menys pietat
com en present dessobre mi pareix.
Tota amor fall, sinó a si mateix;
d'enveja és tot lo món conquistat;
hom sens afany no vol fer algun bé:
com lo farà contra si, ab gran cost?
Cascun cor d'hom io veig pus dur que post;
algú no es dol si altre null mal té.

Lo qui no sap, no pot haver mercè
d'aquell qui jau en turment e dolor;   10
doncs io perdon a cascú de bon cor,
si no són plant del que mon cor sosté.
Secretament, ab no costumat mal,
ventura em fa sa desfavor sentir;
d'Amor no em clam, si bé em porta a morir;
bé i mal passats, io en reste cominal.

Altre socors de vostra amor no em val
sinó que els ulls me demostren voler,
ne res pus cert de vós no puc saber,
ans si més cerc, per ser content no em cal.   20
Io veig molt hom sens amar ser amat,
i el mentidor tant com vol és cregut;
e io d'Amor me trob així vençut,
que dir no pusc quant só enamorat.

Amor, Amor, un hàbit m'he tallat
de vostre drap, vestint-me l'esperit;
en lo vestir, ample molt l'he sentit,
e fort estret, quan sobre mi és posat.

LXXVII

The world cannot show less pity than it has for me at the moment. All love fails, except (for love) of self; the whole world is overrun by envy; no man wants to do good, even when it is no effort: how will he do it despite himself, at great cost? I see that each man's heart is harder than a stump of wood; no one grieves if another suffers injury.

He who does not know (it from experience) cannot feel pity for him who lies in pain and torment; so I pardon everyone with all my heart, if I am not pitied for what my heart is suffering. Secretly, with unaccustomed pain, fortune makes me feel its lack of favour; I do not complain of Love, even though he leads me to death; I remain indifferent to past good and evil.

No other help from your love avails me, unless your eyes show me favour, nor can I know anything more certain about you; indeed, it is unnecessary for me to look for more, in order to be content. I see many men who are loved, without (themselves) being in love, and the liar is believed as much as he wishes; and I find myself so overcome by Love that I cannot say how much I am in love.

O Love, o Love: I cut myself a coat from your cloth, dressing my spirit (in it); when I put it on, I felt it was very large, and (it is) very tight now that I wear it.

LXXIX

Oh vós, mesquins, qui sots terra jaeu
del colp d'Amor ab lo cos sangonent,
e tots aquells qui ab cor molt ardent
han bé amat, prec-vos no us oblideu !
Veniu plorant, ab cabells escampats,
oberts los pits per mostrar vostre cor
com fón plagat ab la sageta d'or
ab què Amor plaga els enamorats.

Los colps d'Amor són per tres calitats,
e veure's pot en les fletxes que fir,   10
per què els ferits són forçats de sentir
dolor del colp segons seran plagats.
D'or e de plom aquestes fletxes són,
e d'un metall que s'anomena argent:
cascú d'aquests dóna son sentiment,
segons que d'ells diferença ha en lo món.

En aquell temps que primer d'aquest fón,
les fletxes d'or Amor totes llançà,
e, desmembrat, una se n'aturà
ab què em ferí, de què viure abandon.   20
De fletxes tals molts passats foren morts;
ja no té pus que fer guerra mortal.
Ab les d'argent sol basta fer senyal,
mas los plagats, de morir són estorts.

Ab les de plom són hui tots sos deports,
e son poder no basta a traure sang.
Amor, veent lo seu poder tan manc,
ha trencat l'arc: io en faç al món reports.
Ab cor sancer crida la sua pau,
per què cascú pot anar en cabells;   30
per fugir d'ell no cal muntar castells,
lo seu poder pus baix que terra jau.

Mas io romanc a mort; d'açò fiau.
La sua pau és guerra per a mi;
si en guerra fos cella per qui em ferí,
io fóra en pau vençut e son esclau.   *over*

LXXIX

O you, wretched ones, who lie underground, your bodies bleeding from the stroke of Love, and all those who, with burning hearts, have loved well, I pray you, do not forget! Come weeping, with dishevelled hair, your breasts open to show how your hearts were pierced by the arrow of gold with which Love wounds those (who are) in love.

The wounds of Love are of three kinds, and this can be seen from the arrows with which he strikes, whence those who are stricken are made to feel pain from their wounds according to the manner in which they are struck. These arrows are of gold and lead, and of a metal which is called silver: each of these conveys its (own) feeling, according to the difference which exists between them on earth.

In times before our own, Love shot all his golden arrows, but thoughtlessly kept just one, with which he wounded me, and so I give up (my) life. By such arrows, many were killed in the past; now Love has no more with which to make war to the death. With those of silver he can only leave a scar, but those whom he wounds are exempted from death.

These days his sport is confined to arrows of lead, and their force is not sufficient to draw blood. Love, seeing his power so feeble, has broken his bow: I announce this to the world. With sincere heart he cries peace, so that all men may go about bareheaded; there is no need to build castles to take refuge from him: his strength lies lower than the earth.

But I lie at death's door: be sure of that. For me, Love's peace is war; if she through whom he wounded me were at war, in peace I would be defeated and her slave.

Pau ha lo món, e guerra io tot sol,
perquè Amor guerrejar ha finit;
io són plagat e no puc ser guarit,
puis la que am, de sa plaga no es dol.   40

Oh folla Amor! Qui vostre delit vol,
sobre lloc fals ha son contentament;
per ço repòs no té en l'enteniment,
car si no el ver l'enteniment no col.

LXXXI

Així com cell qui es veu prop de la mort,
corrent mal temps, perillant en la mar,
e veu lo lloc on se pot restaurar
e no hi ateny per sa malvada sort,
ne pren a mé, qui vaig afanys passant,
e veig a vós bastant mos mals delir.
Desesperat de mos desigs complir,
iré pel món vostre ergull recitant.

LXXXII

Quan plau a Déu que la fusta peresca,
en segur port romp àncores i ormeig,
e de poc mal a molt hom morir veig:
null hom és cert d'algun fet com fenesca.
L'home sabent no té pus avantatge
sinó que el pec sol menys fets avenir.
L'experiment i els juís veig fallir;
Fortuna i Cas los torben llur usatge.

The world is at peace and I alone at war, since Love has ceased to fight; I am wounded and cannot be cured, since she whom I love has no pity for the wound she has caused.

O foolish Love! Whoever desires your pleasure bases his satisfaction on a false ground; thus his understanding has no rest, for the understanding worships only truth.

LXXXI
Like the man who finds himself close to death, when the weather is bad and he is in danger at sea, and sees the place where he could take refuge and by misfortune cannot reach it: so it is with me, who am in trouble, and see that you are sufficient to remedy my cares. Without hope of achieving my desires, I shall go through the world proclaiming your pride.

LXXXII
When it pleases God that the ship should perish, he breaks anchors and tackle in a safe harbour, and I see many people die from trivial ailments: no one is certain how any matter will end. The wise man has no advantage (over the fool), except that the fool is less often right. I see experience and judgement fail; Fortune and Chance disturb their functioning.

LXXXIX

Cervo ferit no desija la font
aitant com io esser a vós present;
al gran repòs de mon contentament
passar no pusc sinó per aquest pont.
Molt me ve tard lo jorn tan desijat,
comprat molt car per dolorós sospir;
e tard o breu só cert que deu venir,
si per la mort camí no m'és tancat.

Esser no pusc d'esperança llançat,
car io us desig segons mon major bé.   10
A vós deman; contra mi res no us té,
mentre el voler vostre em sia donat.
Si el pensament llunyava un sol punt
d'imaginar haver vostre voler,
sens aquell tot, no pusc delit haver;
si no és tot sa, tost porà ser defunt.

Davant me veig de grans dolors un munt,
puis ops he tant per a mon contentar,
e mon voler porà molt menyscabar
si el vostre es mou e no mostra que munt;   20
e devallant, devallarà lo meu,
e, d'alt caent, no darà poc crebant,
car tot extrem altre extrem és donant:
al poc estat no par l'ofensa greu.

Mil veus lo jorn és per mi pregat Déu
de ço que en vós està la major part:
que en mon voler hajau lo vostre esguard;
e prec Amor vos llanç tot poder seu.
E si ho compleix, lladoncs pendreu extrem,
si troba lloc on se prenga en vós;   30
en lloc dispost sa passió és en nós,
e lo contrast tenim e no volem.

Noves de vós saber mortalment tem,
dubtant-me fort que no hi mostreu amor;
per no saber visc en altra dolor:
no sé de qual costat guard que no em crem.   *over*

LXXXIX

The wounded deer does not long for the spring as much as I (long) to be in your presence; only by this bridge can I cross into the great calm of my happiness. The day so much desired comes very slowly to me, so dearly bought with painful sighs; and I am sure that it will come sooner or later, if the road is not closed to me by death.

I cannot be turned away from hope, for I desire you as my greatest good. It is you I ask; nothing holds you back from me as long as I am given your will. If my mind ceases for one moment to imagine that I possess your will, unless (I possess) it entirely, I can have no pleasure; if your will is not completely sound, it can soon be dead.

I see before me a mountain of great suffering, since such a quantity is necessary for my happiness, and my desire may grow much less if yours fluctuates and does not show that it increases; and if it goes downhill, so will my own, and, falling from a height, it will break to pieces, for every extreme leads to its opposite: to the (man of) humble condition no insult seems severe.

A thousand times a day I pray God for what for the most part lies with you: that you may have regard to my desire; and I beg Love to give you all his strength. And if he does this, you will come to the extremity, if there is any place where Love may take root in you; his passion finds in us a fitting place, and, (though) we could oppose it, we do not wish to.

I am mortally afraid to have news of you, greatly fearing that you will not show signs of love; through not knowing, I live in a different (kind of) suffering: in whatever direction I look, I am burned.

No és en vós complir lo meu delit,
per bé que vós vullau complir aquell;
d'amor haveu haver forçat consell,
en vós i en ell recau mon bé complit.   40

Res no temau ne prengau en despit
dels pensaments meus ab varietat,
car en servei seran de fermetat;
de tals servents vol ser Amor servit.
Si punt d'enuig d'est praticar sentiu,
sens amor sou o no sabeu què vol;
ferm lloc no el té qui d'aquest mal se dol,
lo moviment per segurtat teniu.

Si tant de vós com voleu no confiu,
mon gran voler me porta en aquest zel;   50
de vostre cos no tem lo pus prim pèl
que encontra mi res fes ne em fos altiu.
La voluntat vull que pas tota en mi;
io só celós si molt amau a Déu;
dant-vos delit sens mi, lo mal creix meu;
quan vós dolgués, de mal vostre em dolguí.

Mon darrer bé, de vós io guard la fi,
quan de present me trob ésser content,
e si em veig trist per algun cas present,
res venidor trobar no es pot en mi.   60

XCII

Aquelles mans que jamés perdonaren
han ja romput lo fil tenint la vida
de vós, qui sou de aquest món eixida,
segons los fats en secret ordenaren.
Tot quant io veig e sent, dolor me torna,
dant-me record de vós, qui tant amava.
En ma dolor si prim e bé es cercava,
se trobarà que delit s'hi contorna;
doncs, durarà, puis té qui la sostinga,
car sens delit dolor crec no es retinga.   *over*

It is not by your choice (alone) that my pleasure can be fulfilled, even if you were in favour of fulfilling it; you are compelled to take Love's advice: on you and on him depends my perfect good.

Do not fear or take exception to my changing thoughts, since in (your) service they will be firm; Love likes to be waited on by such servants. If you feel in the least offended by such behaviour, you are without love, or do not know what love demands; whoever suffers from this sickness has no resting-place; take (my) instability as (a sign of) constancy.

If I do not have as much faith in you as you would wish, (it is) my great desire (which) drives me to such jealousy; I am not afraid that the slightest hair on your body will act against or scorn me. I want your will to become entirely mine; I am jealous if you love God a great deal; when you take pleasure without me, my misfortune increases; whenever you suffered, I suffered at your misfortune.

My final good: I think of your death whenever I feel content with the present; and if I feel sad because of some present instance, nothing future is to be found in me.

XCII

Those hands which never pardoned have now broken the thread which held the life of you who have left this world, as the fates secretly decreed. All that I see and feel turns to grief, reminding me of you, whom I loved so much. In my suffering, if one looks closely, one will find that pleasure is mixed with it; therefore my suffering will endure, since it has something to sustain it, for, without pleasure, I believe suffering does not remain.

En cor gentil Amor per mort no passa,
mas en aquell qui per los vicis tira;
la quantitat d'amor durar no mira.
la qualitat d'amor bona no es lassa.
Quan l'ull no veu e lo toc no es pratica,
mor lo voler, que tot per ells se guanya;
qui en tal punt és, dolor sent molt estranya,
mas dura poc: l'expert ho testifica.
Amor honest los sants amants fa colre:
d'aquest vos am, e Mort no.l me pot tolre.   20

Tots los volers que en mi confusos eren,
se mostren clar per llur obra forana:
ma carn se dol, car sa natura ho mana,
perquè en la Mort sos delits se perderen;
en sa dolor ma arma és embolcada,
de què llur plor e plant per null temps callen.
En tal dolor tots los conhorts me fallen,
com, sens tornar, la que am és anada.
Mas l'altra amor, de amistança pura,
aprés sa mort, sa força gran li dura.   30

Aquesta amor, si los pecs no la creen,
és ver senyal del bé que en ella habita:
aquesta és qui sens dolor delita,
i els cecs volers de prop aquesta es veen.
Lo voler cec del tot ella il.lumena,
mas no en tant que lleve el cataracte,
e si pusqués fer sens empatx son acte,
no fóra al món ull ab gota serena;
mas és així com la poca triaga,
que molt verí sa virtut li apaga.   40

Aquell voler que en ma carn sola es causa,
si no és mort, no tardarà que muira;
l'altre per qui dol continu m'abuira,
si em defalleix, no serà sens gran causa.
Ell pot ser dit voler concupiscible,
e sol durar, puis molt de l'arma toca,
mas fall per temps, car virtut no invoca,
e d'un costat és apetit sensible.   *over*

In a noble heart, Love does not undergo death, but (only) in that which is inclined to vices; the quantity of love has no hope of lasting, the quality of good love never tires. When the eye does not see and touch is not practised, the desire which arises entirely from these (senses) dies; anyone who is in such a state feels a strange grief, but this does not last long: the experienced man confirms this. Honest love leads to the cult of saintly lovers: I love you with such a love, and Death cannot take it away from me.

All the desires which were confused in me are shown clearly by their outward behaviour: my flesh suffers, since its nature decrees it, because its pleasures are lost in Death; in its suffering my soul is involved, so that the tears and lamentations of both are never silent. In such suffering all comforts fail me, for she whom I love is gone, and will not come back. But the other love, that of pure friendship, its great strength endures after her death.

This love, though fools do not believe it, is a true sign of the good which resides in it: it is this (love) which gives joy without suffering, and in its presence blind desires can see. It gives light to blind desire, though not so completely that it removes its cataract, and if it could act without hindrance, no eye in the world would be impaired; but it is like the insufficient antidote whose power is cancelled by too much poison.

That desire which arises from my flesh alone, if it is not dead, will not be long in dying; that other (desire) by which I am watered with continual suffering, if it fails in me, it will not be without great cause. It may be called concupiscible desire, and generally lasts, since it greatly concerns the soul, but it fails in time, since it does not call upon virtue, and in part is sensual appetite.

Aquests volers l'amor honesta em torben,
perquè entre mal e bé mes penses orben.   50

D'arma e cos és compost l'hom, contraris,
per què el voler e l'apetit contrasten;
tot quant aquests de llur natura tasten
és saborós e vitals lletovaris.
Altre voler que en mig d'aquests camina,
és atrobat que no té via certa;
cuida haver port en la platja deserta,
e lo verí li sembla medecina.
Aquest voler ab arma i cos conversa,
naix d'ells e fa la obra d'ells diversa.   60

Tres són les parts vers on mos volers pugen,
e per semblant vénen per tres maneres;
entre si han contràries carreres,
delits portants e d'altres que m'enugen.
Quan los delits del cos la pensa em mostra,
io sent dolor car són perduts sens cobre.
Altra dolor sent que em vist tot e em cobre,
com pens que Mort ha tolta l'amor nostra.
L'altre voler raó i natura funden,
que sens dolor molts delits ne abunden.   70

Lo lloc on jau la dolor gran que passe,
no és del tot fora de mes natures,
ne del tot és fora de llurs clausures;
lo moviment creu que per elles passe.
Aquell voler que en mi no troba terme
és lo mijà per on dolor m'agreuja;
l'extrem d'aquest fora natura alleuja,
fort e punyent, mas encansable verme.
Opinió falsa per tots és dita,
que fora nós e dintre nós habita.   80

D'aquesta amor les demés gents tremolen;
aquesta és sentida i no sabuda;
poques gents han sa causa coneguda;
delits, dolors per ella venir solen.
Lo cos per si lo seu delit desija,   *over*

These desires disturb honest love in me, since, between good and evil, they blind my thoughts.

Man is composed of soul and body, which are contraries, so that will and appetite conflict; everything the body and soul taste naturally is a pleasant, life-giving medicine. Another desire, which makes its way between the two, is found to have no sure road; it thinks it will find haven on a deserted beach and poison seems to it a remedy. This desire communicates with soul and body; it is born of them and performs their separate actions.

There are three parts towards which my desires mount, and similarly they arise in three ways; they take different courses from one another, bringing pleasures and other feelings which trouble me. When my thoughts show me the pleasures of the body, I feel sorrow, since they are lost beyond recall. I feel a different sorrow which clothes and covers me completely, when I think that Death has taken away our love. Reason and nature create this other desire, for great joys do not abound without suffering.

The place where lies the great suffering I experience is not entirely beyond my own natures, nor is it entirely beyond their confines; I believe that the motive (for my suffering) passes through them. That (other) desire which in me has no limit is the means by which my suffering is increased: its opposite lies outside nature, a strong and piercing, but relentless, worm. A wrong opinion is voiced by people in general, since it dwells both outside and inside us.

Most people tremble at this kind of love; it is felt and not understood; few have known its cause; joys and sufferings usually come from it. The body in itself desires its pleasure;

l'arma enaprés lo sent, e vol atènyer
lo propri seu, al qual no es pot empènyer,
car tot és fals, d'on ella se fastija.
D'aquests contrasts aquesta amor escapa,
que veritat no ateny ab sa capa.   90

Tant és unit lo cos ab la nostra arma,
que acte en l'hom no pot ser dit bé simple;
algú no és vers l'altre humil e simple:
contrast se fan, u contra l'altre s'arma.
Mas és tan poc lo contrast a sa hora,
que en fets del cos l'arma no fa gran nosa;
i en contemplant, així l'arma reposa,
que, bé reprès, lo cos d'açò no plora.
Aquesta pau en mi no és molt llonga,
per què dolor més que el delit s'allonga.   100

Dolor io sent e sembla a mi extrema;
no só en punt de voler consell rebre,
e de negun remei me vull percebre,
ans de tristor he presa ja ma tema.
Si em trob en punt que dolor no m'acorde,
ja tinc senyal ab què a dolor torne:
record sos fets d'amor, e allens borne;
d'ací scapant ab oci no em concorde.
Son esperit ab lo cos io contemple;
tant delit sent com l'hom devot al temple.   110

De pietat de sa mort ve que em dolga,
e só forçat que mon mal haja a plànyer;
tant he perdut, que bé no em pot atànyer,
Fortuna ja no té què pus me tolga.
Quan imagín les voluntats unides
i el conversar, separats per a sempre,
pensar no puc ma dolor haja tempre,
mes passions no trob gens aflaquides;
e si per temps elles passar havien,
vengut és temps que començar devien.   120

Mes voluntats mos pensaments aporten
avall i amunt, sí com los núvols l'aire;   *over*

later the soul feels it and wants to achieve its own pleasure, which it lacks the power to obtain, for it is entirely false, and this vexes the soul. This kind of love avoids these conflicts, since its extent does not reach to truth.

The body is so united with the soul that no action in man can ever be called single; neither is humble and simple towards the other: they conflict and take up arms against one another. But the conflict is so small when they act separately that, in the body's actions, the soul is no great obstacle; and, in contemplation, the soul rests in such a way that the body, well-restrained, sheds no tears at this. This peace in me does not last very long, since suffering endures longer than pleasure.

I feel grief and it seems to me extreme; I am not in a state to wish to receive advice and I do not want to see any remedy: rather have I taken my theme from sadness. If I find myself at a stage where I do not remember my grief, I already have a sign that I shall return to it: I remember her acts of love, and more vividly than before; I do not consent to escape from this into peace of mind. I contemplate both her spirit and her body; I feel joy as great as that of the pious man in church.

Out of pity I come to grieve for her death and I am compelled to lament my misfortune; I have lost so much that no good can reach me: Fortune has no more to take away from me. When I imagine our united wills and our conversation, now separated for ever, I cannot think my grief will ever know moderation: I do not find my sufferings have decreased at all; and if some day they were to pass, the time for this to begin has now arrived.

My feelings drive my thoughts up and down like clouds in the air;

adés me dolc, puis dolor no sent gaire,
e sent dolors que ab si delits comporten.
Quan pens que els morts de res dels vius no pensen
e les dolors que pas sens grat se perden,
mos sentiments han mal, e no s'esperden
tant que d'amor e dolor se defensen;
e pas dolor que en la d'infern s'acosta,
com en est món no la'm veuré de costa.   130

En altre món a mi par que io sia
i els propis fets estranys a mi aparen;
semblant d'aquells que mos juís loaren,
lo fals par ver, la veritat falsia.
Los meus juís la dolor los ofega,
lo lloc no hi és on primer habitaven.
Si és, no tal com ans del cas estaven;
alterat és: la Mort. I açò em fa brega
tal e tan fort, que altre matant, mi mata.
No sé com és que lo cor no m'esclata.   140

Alguns han dit que la Mort és amarga;
poden-ho dir los qui la sabor senten,
o de per si o com per altre tenten
sa fort dolor, que entre totes és llarga.
Per mi no tem, per altre l'he temuda;
puis fón cruel, ja pietat no m'haja;
qui en terra jau, no tem pus avall caja:
en l'esperat ma sperança és perduda.
O partiment dolorós, perdurable,
fent en dolor mi comparat diable!   150

No preu los béns que io sol posseesca,
car plaent res home sol no pratica;
la Mort no tem, que lo món damnifica,
sinó que tem que el cel me defallesca.
Tot cas io mir ab una egual cara:
res no em fa trist, e ja, molt més, alegre;
no és color dessobre, blanc o negre:
vers mi no hi ha cosa scura ne clara.
Tot quant Amor e Por me pogren noure,
finí lo jorn que li viu los ulls cloure.   *over*

at times I grieve, at others I scarcely feel pain, and I feel sufferings which bring pleasures with them. When I reflect that the dead do not think at all of the living, and the grief which I endure without reward will disappear, my feelings suffer, and will not go away unless they reject both love and grief; and I go through pains like those of Hell because in this world I shall never see her at my side.

I seem to live in another world, and my own actions seem strange to me; like those actions which my own opinions praised, the false seems true (and) truth false. Grief stifles my opinions: the place where they used to dwell is no longer there. If it *is* there, they are not as before the event; it is changed: (by) Death. And Death attacks so fiercely and in such a way that, in killing another, she kills me. I do not know why my heart does not burst.

Some have said that Death is bitter; those who experience her taste may say this, or who themselves or through others sample her great pain, which lasts longer than any other. I do not fear Death for myself: I have feared her for another; since she has been cruel, let her show no pity for me; whoever lies in the earth is not afraid to fall still further: my hope in what I hoped is lost. O painful, final parting, making me equal in suffering to the devil!

I do not value the goods which I alone possess, for a man does not perform pleasant things on his own; I do not fear Death, whom everyone curses, but fear that Heaven may escape me. I look on all things with an equal countenance: nothing makes me sad, still less happy; there is no colour left, white or black: for me, nothing is dark or light. All injuries that Love or Fear could do me came to an end on the day when I saw her close her eyes.

Segons lo cas ma dolor no és tanta
com se requer per un mortal damnatge;
sobre tots mals la Mort porta avantatge:
io l'he sentit e de present m'espanta.
Segons l'Amor, del dany no port gran signe,
e volgra io que en lo món fos notable,
dient cascú:—Veus l'home pus amable—,
e que plangués cascú mon fat maligne.
Aquell voler causat per cosa honesta,
mentre seré, serà mostrant gran gesta.   170

Tan comun cas, ¿ per què tan extrem sembla
al qui per sort la Mort en tant lo plaga?
¿ Per què en tal cas la raó d'hom s'amaga,
e passió tota sa força assembla?
Déu piadós e just cruel se mostra:
tant és en nós torbada coneixença!
Fluixant dolor, primer plega creença,
mas ferm saber no és en potença nostra.
Als que la Mort toll la muller aimia
sabran jutjar part de la dolor mia.   180

Tot ver amic a son ver amic ama
de tal amor que Mort no la menyscaba,
ans és fornal que apura l'or i acaba,
lleixant-lo fi, e l'àls en fum derrama.
D'aquest amor am aquella qui és morta,
e, tement, am tot quant és de aquella.
L'esperit viu. Doncs, ¿ quina maravella
que am aquell? E res tant no em conforta.
Membra'm la Mort, e torn en ma congoixa,
e quant hi só, dolor pas com me floxa.   190

Accident és Amor, e no substança,
e per sos fets se dóna a nós conèixer;
quant és ne qual ell se dóna a parèixer;
segons d'on part, així sa força llança.
Sí com lo vent, segons les encontrades
on és passat, de si cald o fred gita,
així Amor dolor da o delita,   *over*

To all appearances, my suffering is not as great as a mortal injury entails; Death has the advantage over all (other) evils: I have experienced this (in another's death) and now it terrifies me. In terms of Love, I bear no great signs of injury, and I wish it were more obvious to other people, so that everyone would say: 'Behold the greatest lover of all', and each one pity my evil fate. That desire which comes from an honest cause will give rise to noble actions as long as I live.

Why does such a common case seem so extreme to one who by chance is so stricken by Death? Why, in such a case, does one's reason hide and passion assemble all its forces? God, who is pitying and just, shows himself to be cruel: so confused is our knowledge of Him! When suffering decreases, faith is the first thing to return, but firm knowledge is not within our power. Those from whom Death has taken away the woman they loved will be able to judge part of my suffering.

Every true friend loves his (own) true friend with a love such that Death does not diminish it; rather is Death a crucible which refines and perfects gold, leaving it pure, and scatters the rest in smoke. With such a love I love her who is dead, and, in my fear, I love everything that had to do with her. The spirit lives. Then, what wonder I love it? And nothing consoles me so much. I am reminded of Death, and I return to my grief, and when I do so, I suffer pain which weakens me.

Love is an accident and not a substance, and makes himself known to us through his actions; he does not reveal his quantity or his quality; according to where he starts from, so he projects his strength. Just as the wind, depending on the region through which it has passed, sends out warmth or cold, so Love gives suffering or joy,

segons lo for del lloc on ha llançades
fondes raïls: o sus cara de terra,
o sobre fang, o sus molt aspra serra.   200

Amor en l'hom dos llocs disposts atroba,
car hom és dit per ses dues natures:
lo cos per si vol semblant de sutzures,
l'arma per si d'un blanc net vol sa roba.
D'ells aunits surt amor, d'algun acte
que no es diu bé qual d'ells més part hi faça;
cascú per si algun delit acaça,
i, aquell atès, l'altre en porta caràcter.
E veus la Mort que llur voler termena:
lo bo no pot, no basta que l'ofena.   210

Morint lo cos, a son amant no el resta
sinó dolor, per lo record del plaure;
fallint aquell, no tarda amor en caure:
fallint lo sant, defall la sua festa.
Alguns delits que en l'arma pel cos vénen,
són los composts que els amadors turmenten,
e cascú d'ells tanta i qual dolor senten
segons del cos o de l'arma part prenen;
e, mort l'amat, amor és duradora
tant quant lo mort del viu té gran penyora.   220

Ço que en passat envolt e confús era,
és departit: lo gra no és ab la palla;
experiment altre no em pens hi valla;
per la Mort és oberta la carrera.
Ma carn no sent; doncs no es pot fer que ame,
car ja no és ço que sentir hi feia;
si voler tinc, pec és lo qui no creia
que l'esperit de pura amor s'enflame,
cobejant molt que Déu sa arma s'emporte;
açò dubtant, que io pena reporte.   230

Si en nostra amor pens ésser fi venguda
e d'ella perd esperança de veure,
sinó que tost vinc en açò descreure,
l'arma en lo cos no fora retenguda.   *over*

according to the law of the place where it has thrust out its deep roots: on the earth's surface, or on mud, or on the rough mountain.

Love finds two places prepared for him in man, for man is defined by his two natures: the body on its own desires the appearance of filth; the soul by itself wishes its clothing (to be) of pure white. Love proceeds from both together, from an act which does not make it clear which of the two has the greater share in it; each seeks for some pleasure on its own account and, having achieved it, the other bears its imprint. And you see that Death puts an end to their desires; (but) she cannot end what is good, however much she offends it.

When the body dies, nothing is left to the one who loved it except grief at the memory of pleasure; when this fails, love is not long in declining: when the saint fails, his feast day lapses. Those pleasures which come to the soul by way of the body are the compound actions which torment lovers, and each feels such pain, of such a kind, according to the extent to which they share in the body or the soul; and when the loved one dies, love lasts for as long as the dead one retains the pledge of the living.

What in the past was tangled and confused has gone: the grain is no longer with the straw; no other experience, I think, is of any value; the way has been cleared by Death. I do not feel my flesh; then it is impossible for it to love, since that which made it feel no longer exists; if I have any desire, he is a fool who does not believe that my spirit burns with pure love, keenly desiring that God should take her soul to himself; if I doubt this, may I suffer for it.

If I believe an end has come to our love, and I lose hope of seeing her again, unless I soon abandon this belief, may my soul not remain in my body.

Si bé los morts en lo món no retornen,
ans de ser mort noves sabré d'aquella.
Stat és ja: doncs, no es gran meravella,
açò sperant, mos sentiments sojornen;
e si cert fos que entre los sants fos mesa,
no volgra io que de Mort fos defesa.   240

O Déu, mercè! Mas no sé de què et pregue,
sinó que mi en lo seu lloc aculles;
no em tardes molt que dellà mi no vulles,
puis l'esperit on és lo seu aplegue;
e lo meu cos, ans que la vida fine,
sobre lo seu abraçat vull que jaga.
Ferí'ls Amor de no curable plaga;
separà'ls Mort: dret és que ella els veïne.
Lo jorn del Jui, quan pendrem carn e ossos,
mescladament partirem nostres cossos.   250

XCIV

Puis me trob sol en amor, a mi sembla
que en mi tot ço sia costum estranya:
amor se perd entre gents per absença,
e per la mort la mia amor no fina,
ans molt més am a vós en mort que en vida,
e io perdon si algú no em vol creure:
pocs són aquells qui altres coses creguen
sinó semblants d'aquelles que els avenen.

Ma dolor fort lo comun córs no serva;
tota dolor lo temps la venç e gasta;   10
no dic que en tot a tota altra dessemble:
en quantitat molt prop d'altres se jutja;
en qualitat ab les altres discorda.
Seguint l'Amor d'on ella pren sa forma,
gran part del temps seca dolor me dóna
i algun delit ab altra dolor dolça.

Dins lo cos d'hom les humors se discorden;
de temps en temps llur poder se transmuda: *over*

Though the dead do not return to earth, before I die, I shall have news of her. It has already happened: then it is no great wonder that my feelings remain in hope of this; and if it were certain that she had been placed among the saints, I should not want her to be protected from Death.

O mercy, God! But I do not know what to beg of you, except that you (should) gather me to her place; do not delay long in wishing me in the next world, (and) therefore take my spirit where her own resides; and, before my life ends, I wish my body to lie with its arms around hers. Love dealt them an incurable wound; Death separated them: it is right that she should bring them together. On the Day of Judgement, when we take on flesh and bone, we shall share out our bodies without distinction.

XCIV

Because I am unique in love, it seems to me as if everything in me were a strange custom: among other people, love is lost through absence, and my own love does not end with death; indeed, I love you much more in death than in life, and I forgive those who will not believe me: there are few who believe things other than those which happen to themselves.

My great suffering does not follow the normal course; all suffering is conquered and diminished by time; I do not say that my own is utterly different from any other kind (of suffering): in quantity it considers itself very similar to others; in quality it is different. Following Love, from which it takes its form, most of the time it gives me sterile grief and occasional pleasure with another, (more) gentle kind of suffering.

Within man's body, the humours disagree; from time to time their power varies:

en un sols jorn regna malenconia,
n'aquell mateix còlera, sang e fleuma.   20
Tot enaixí les passions de l'arma
mudament han molt divers o contrari,
car en un punt per ella es fan los actes,
e prestament és en lo cos la causa.

Així com l'or que de la mena el traen
està mesclat de altres metalls sútzeus,
e, mès al foc, en fum se'n va la lliga,
lleixant l'or pur no podent-se corrompre,
així la Mort mon voler gros termena:
aquell fermat en la part contrassemble   30
d'aquella que la Mort al món l'ha tolta,
l'honest voler en mi roman sens mescla.

Dos volers són que natura segueixen,
e cascú d'ells l'hom per natura guien;
sí acte ensems fan mal o bé atracen
segons qual d'ells en l'altre ha domini.
Quan la raó l'apetit senyoreja,
és natural de l'hom tota sa obra,
e lo revers sa natura li torba,
e no ateny la fi que en tots fets cerca.   40

Quan l'apetit segueix la part de l'arma,
l'home va dret, seguint natura mestra,
car la major part la remor se tira
e ves la fi que va lo camí troba;
e l'apetit volent son necessari,
l'home no fall, si no trespassa l'orde,
e si s'estén més que natura dicta,
surt-ne voler fals, opinionàtic.

Les voluntats que per natura vénen,
en certitud e terme són compreses.   50
L'altre voler passa d'hom les natures;
son senyal cert és que no l'enclou terme.
De tots aquests passions mantengueren
mescladament, sí com mesclats jaïen;
mas bé distints són aprés de son obte,
e separats los sent, quasi visibles.

over

in a single day, melancholy reigns, and in that same day, choler, blood and phlegm. In the same way, the passions of the soul go through very different or contrary changes, for in one instant actions are performed by the soul and immediately the cause is in the body.

Like gold which, (when) they extract it from the mine, is mixed with other base metals, and, placed in the fire, the dross goes off in smoke, leaving pure gold which cannot be corrupted, so Death puts an end to my base appetite: this was enclosed in the bodily part of her whom Death has taken away from earth, (and) honest desire remains in me unmixed.

There are two desires which follow nature, and each of them guides man naturally; when they act together, they perform good or evil according to which of them dominates the other. When reason controls the appetite, its whole operation is worthy of man, and the reverse disturbs man's nature and he does not achieve the end which he seeks in all his actions.

When appetite follows the soul's part, man goes straight, following nature, his mentor; for the greater part attracts the lesser and finds the way which leads to his true end; and when the appetite desires what is necessary to it, man does not fall into error, as long as he does not break the rules, and if he goes beyond what nature decrees, the result is false and inconstant desire.

The impulses which come from nature are contained in limits and certainty. The other desire exceeds human nature; its sure sign is that no boundary encloses it. (My) passions kept all these desires in confusion, just as the desires themselves lay mixed together; but since her death, they are quite distinct, and I feel them separately, as if they were visible.

Molts són al món que mos dits no entengueren
e ja molts més que d'aquells no sentiren.
¿ Qui creure pot que entre amors vicioses
voler honest treball per estar simple,   60
gitant de si meravellós efecte
estant secret per força dels contraris ?
Dolç i agre ensems, llur sabor no és distinta;
ella vivint, mos volers aitals foren.

Dolre's del mort ve de amor comuna,
e de açò io em sent tot lo damnatge:
fugir les gents quisque sien alegres
i haver despit que jamés lo dol fine.
Tot delit fuig com a cosa enemiga
car un bé poc entre grans mals dol porta,   70
e met poder que em torn dolor en hàbit,
perquè de goig la sabor jamés taste.

Senyals d'amor que en tal cas hòmens senten,
jo trob en mi que sens dolor se prenen:
si res començ, io en corromp lo principi,
per què la fi de res mi no contenta.
Molt e pus fort tota amor me da fàstic,
e sembla a mi ser cosa abominable;
si algun delit entre mes dolors mescle,
de fet lo perd e torn a ma congoixa.   80

Si el pensament per força a altra part llance,
d'ell acordant, ab gran sospir lo cobre;
en lo començ ab dolor en mi entra,
no passa molt que m'és dolor plaïble.
Decrepitud ma natura demostra,
car tota carn a vòmit me provoca;
grans amadors per llur aimia morta
són mi semblants en part, al tot no basten.

Si res io veig d'ella, dolor me dóna,
e si en defuig, par que d'ella m'aparte;   90
los temps e llocs ab lo dit la'm senyalen,
segons en ells delits o dolors foren;   *over*

There are many on earth who have not understood my writings, and many more who have never heard of them. Who can believe that, among shameful loves, an honest desire should struggle to be alone, pouring forth the marvellous effect which had been hidden by the power of contraries? Sweet and bitter at once, their flavour is not separate; while she was alive, such were my desires.

To mourn for the dead person comes from mutual love, and I feel the full pain of this: (which is) to avoid all people who are happy and to resent that suffering should ever end. I avoid all pleasure as a hostile thing, for one small good among great ills brings (more) pain, and I strive that suffering should become a habit, so that I may never again know the taste of joy.

The signs of love which men feel in such a situation, I find affect me without pain: whatever I undertake, I spoil it at the beginning, so that the end of anything does not satisfy me. Much more than this, all love repels me and seems to me an abominable thing; if I mix any pleasure with my sufferings, I immediately lose it and return to my anguish.

If by force I direct my thought elsewhere, remembering it, I recover it with much sighing; at first it enters into me with suffering, (but) before long it is a pleasant pain. My nature shows decrepitude, for all flesh makes me vomit; great lovers who lost the woman they loved are like me in part, but are not altogether equal.

If I see anything of hers, it gives me pain, and if I avoid it, it is as if I were parting from her; times and places point to her with their fingers, according to whether suffering or pleasure occurred there;

e són-ne tals que la'm demostren trista,
altres, e molts, mostrants aquella alegra.
E pas dolor com jamés li fiu greuge,
e volgra açò ab la mia sang rembre.

Amor és dat conèixer pels efectes.
Sa cantitat no té mesura certa:
gran és o poc l'amador segons altre,
e poder pren Amor, segons on entra.   100
La qualitat és tal com segons guarda,
car de semblants és forçat que s'engendre;
la carn vol carn, l'arma son semblant cerca,
d'ells neix fill bord als engenrants contrari.

Qui ama carn, perduda carn, no ama,
mas en membrant lo delit, dol li resta.
En tot amor cau amat e amable;
doncs, mort lo cos, aquell qui ell amava
no pot amar, no trobant res que ame.
Amor no viu, desig mort i esperança,   110
i en lo no res no pot haver espera;
quant és del cos, la Mort a no res torna.

Si la que am és fora d'aquest segle,
la major part d'aquella és en ésser.
E quan al món en carn ella vivia,
son esperit io volguí amar simple:
e doncs, ¿ quant més que en present res no em torba ?
Ella vivint, la carn m'era rebel.le;
los grans contrasts de nostres parts discordes
canten, forçats, acord, e de grat, contra.   120

De mon voler jutge cascú la causa,
e farà poc veent en mi les obres;
la mia amor per la Mort no és morta,
ne sent dolor, veent-me lo món perdre.
Io am, e tem ab honesta vergonya,
l'esperit sol de la qui Déus perdone,
e res de mi ne del món no cobege
sinó que Déu en lo cel la col.loque.   *over*

and there are some which recall her to me in sadness and others—many—which show her as happy. And it hurts me to think that I ever offended her, and I should like to redeem this with my blood.

Love is known by its effects. Its quantity has no certain measure: the lover is greater or lesser in someone else's opinion, and Love assumes power, depending on where it enters. Quality varies according to what it beholds, for it is born inevitably from likenesses; flesh desires flesh, soul seeks its like: from the one and the other is born an illegitimate child, contrary to its parents.

Whoever loves the flesh, once the flesh is lost, ceases to love, but, remembering the pleasure, he is left with pain. In every love there is a lover and a beloved; so, once the body is dead, he who loved the body cannot love, since he finds nothing to love. Love does not live when desire and hope are dead, and in nothingness there can be no hope; whatever belongs to the body, Death turns (it) to nothing.

If she whom I love has left this world, her greater part still survives. And when she lived on earth in the flesh, I wanted to love her spirit alone: then, how much more so, now that nothing hinders me? While she was alive, my flesh rebelled against me; the great differences between our discordant parts sing in harmony, now they are compelled to, though (when they were) free, (they pulled) against one another.

Let every man judge the cause of my desire, and he will easily observe the results in me; my love has not been killed by Death, nor do I feel grief at losing the world. I love and fear with honest shame the spirit alone of her whom God forgive, and I desire nothing of myself or of the world except that God may set her in Heaven.

Mare de Déu, si és en purgatori
son esperit per no purgats delictes,   130
sí ton Fill prec no guard los precs d'on vénen,
mas lla on van. Mos pecats no li noguen!

XCVI

La gran dolor que llengua no pot dir
del qui es veu mort e no sap on irà
(no sap son Déu si per a si el volrà
o si en l'infern lo volrà sebollir):
semblant dolor lo meu esperit sent,
no sabent què de vós Déus ha ordenat,
car vostre bé o mal a mi és dat,
del que haureu jo en seré sofirent.

Tu, esperit, qui has fet partiment
ab aquell cos qual he io tant amat,   10
veges a mi qui só passionat,
dubtant estic fer-te raonament.
Lo lloc on est me farà canviar
d'enteniment de ço que et volré dir;
goig o tristor per tu he io complir,
en tu està quant Déu me volrà dar.

Pregant a Déu, les mans no em cal plegar,
car fet és tot quant li pot avenir:
si és al cel, no es pot lo bé spremir;
si en infern, en foll és mon pregar.   20
Si és així, anul.la'm l'esperit,
sia tornat mon ésser en no-res,
e majorment si en lloc tal per mi és;
no sia io de tant adolorit.

No sé què dir que em fartàs d'haver dit;
si crid o call, no trob qui em satisfés;
si vag o pens, he temps en va despès;
de tot quant faç, ans de fer me penit.
No planc lo dany de mon delit perdut,
tanta és la por que em ve de son gran mal!   *over*

Mother of God, if her spirit is in Purgatory for unexpiated sins, I pray your Son not to consider where the prayers come from, but where they are going to. May my sins not harm her!

XCVI

The great suffering which no tongue can describe of him who is dead and does not know where he will go (he does not know whether his God will want him for Himself, or whether He will bury him in Hell): my spirit suffers equally, not knowing what God has decreed for you, for your salvation or doom is given (also) to me: whichever you are allotted, I (too) shall suffer it.

You, spirit, who have departed from that body which I loved so much, look at me in my suffering: I hesitate to speak to you. The place where you are will make me change my mind concerning what I would say to you; through you I shall receive joy or sadness; whatever God wishes to give me lies in you.

I do not need to join my hands in prayer to God, since all that can happen to her is decided: if she is in Heaven, such good cannot be expressed; if in Hell, my prayer is foolish. If it is the latter, cancel my spirit, let my being return to nothingness, the more so if she is in such a place because of me; let me not suffer such anguish.

I do not know what to say that I should not regret having said; whether I cry out or remain silent, I find nothing to satisfy me; whether I let my mind wander or concentrate my thoughts, it is a waste of time; whatever I do, I regret before I do it. I do not mourn the injury of my lost delight, so great is the fear which comes from her great misfortune!

Tot mal és poc si no és perpetual,
e tem aquest no l'haja merescut.

Lo dany mortal és molt més que temut,
e tol-ne part ésser a tots egual.
O tu, Dolor, sies-me cominal!;
encontra oblit vulles-me ser escut!
Fir-me lo cor e tots los senys me pren,
farta't en mi, car no em defens de tu,
dóna'm tant mal que me'n planga cascú;
tant com tu pots, lo teu poder m'estén.   40

Tu, esperit, si res no te'n defèn,
romp lo costum que dels morts és comú;
torna en lo món e mostra què és de tu:
lo teu esguard no em donarà spavent.

XCVII

Si per null temps creguí ser amador,
en mi conec d'amor poc sentiment.
Si mi compar al comú de la gent,
és veritat que en mi trob gran amor;
però si guard algú del temps passat
i el que Amor pot fer en lloc dispost,
nom d'amador solament no m'acost,
car tant com dec no só passionat.

Morta és ja la que tant he amat,
mas io són viu, veent ella morir;   10
ab gran amor no es pot bé soferir
que de la Mort me pusca haver llunyat.
Lla dec anar on és lo seu camí,
no sé què em té que en açò no m'acord:
sembla que ho vull, mas no és ver, puis Mort
res no la toll al qui la vol per si.

Enquer està que vida no finí,
com prop la mort io la viu acostar,
dient plorant:—No vullau mi lleixar,
hajau dolor de la dolor de mi!—   *over*

Any misfortune is small if it is not eternal, but I fear she may not have earned this kind.

The pain of death is much more than feared, and this is partly because it is common to all men. O Grief, be impartial to me!; be a shield to me against oblivion! Wound my heart and capture all my senses, do as you like with me, for I do not defend myself against you: grant me so much misfortune that everyone pities me; as much as you are able, extend your power over me.

You, spirit, if nothing prevents you from it, break the custom which is common to the dead; come back to earth and show what has become of you: your look will not cause me terror.

XCVII

If at any time I thought myself a lover, I can recognize little feeling of love in myself. If I compare myself to the majority of people, it is true that I find great love within me; but if I consider any (lover) from the past and what Love can do in a place which is prepared (for it), I simply cannot aspire to the name of lover, for I am not as passionate as I should be.

She whom I have loved so much is now dead, but I am alive, having seen her die; with great love, it is hard to accept that I have escaped Death. I ought to go where her road lies: I do not know what prevents me from deciding to do this; it looks as if I wanted to, but it is not true, since nothing takes Death away from him who wishes it for himself.

(Her) life had still not come to an end when I saw her draw near to death, saying with tears: 'Please do not leave me, have pity on my suffering!'

O cor malvat d'aquell qui es veu tal cas,
com pecejat o sens sang no roman!
Molt poca amor e pietat molt gran
degra bastar que senyal gran mostràs.

¿ Qui serà aquell que en dolre abastàs
lo piadós mal de la Mort vengut?
O cruel mal, qui tolls la joventut
e fas podrir les carns dins en lo vas!
L'esperit, ple de paor, volant va
a l'incert lloc, tement l'eternal dany;   30
tot lo delit present deçà roman.
Qui és lo sant qui de Mort no dubtà?

¿ Qui serà aquell qui la mort planyerà,
d'altre o de si, tant com és lo gran mal?
Sentir no es pot lo damnatge mortal,
molt menys lo sap qui mort jamés temptà.
O cruel mal, donant departiment
per tots los temps als coratges units!
Mos sentiments me trob esbalaïts,
mon esperit no té son sentiment.   40

Tots mos amics hajen complanyiment
de mi, segons veuran ma passió;
haja delit lo meu fals companyó,
e l'envejós, qui de mal delit sent,
car tant com puc, io em dolc e dolre'm vull,
e com no em dolc, assats pas desplaer,
car io desig que perdés tot plaer
e que jamés cessàs plorar mon ull!

Tan poc no am que ma cara no mull
d'aigua de plor, sa vida i mort pensant;   50
en tristor visc, de sa vida membrant,
e de sa mort aitant com puc me dull.
No bast en més, en mi no puc fer pus,
sinó obeir lo que ma dolor vol;
ans perdre vull la raó, si la'm tol,
mas puis no muir, de poca amor m'acús.   *over*

O wretched heart of him who finds himself in such a situation, since it is not broken into pieces or left without blood! Little love and great pity should be enough for it to show great signs.

Who would be equal to mourning the pious injury which comes from Death? O cruel evil which takes away youth and makes the flesh rot in the tomb! The spirit, full of fear, flies off to the uncertain place, afraid of eternal damnation; all present pleasure is left behind. What saint was not afraid of Death?

Who will mourn for death, his own or another's, such is the great evil? One cannot feel the mortal injury; he whom death never tempted knows still less of it. O cruel evil, for ever separating hearts (which were) united! I find my feelings stupefied; my spirit has lost its feeling.

All my friends may pity me when they see my suffering; let my false companion feel pleasure, and the envious one, who takes delight in misfortune, for as much as I am able, I mourn and wish to mourn, and when I do not, I am displeased enough, for I wish to lose all pleasure and that my eyes would never stop weeping!

I do not love so little that no tears wet my face when I think of her life and death; I live in sadness, remembering her life, and I mourn her death as best I can. I cannot do more: all I can do is obey what my grief demands. I would rather lose my reason if it (i.e. grief) takes it away from me, but since I do not die, I accuse myself of little love.

Tot amador d'amar poc no s'escús
que sia viu, e mort lo seu amat,
o que almenys del món visca apartat,
que solament haja nom de reclús.   60

CI

Lo viscaí qui es troba en Alemanya,
paralitic, que no pot senyalar,
si és malalt, remei no li pot dar
metge del món, si doncs no és d'Espanya,
qui del seu mal haurà més coneixença
i entendrà molt millor sa qualitat.
Atal sóc io en estrany lloc posat,
que altre sens vós ja no em pot dar valença.

Io viu uns ulls haver tan gran potença
de dar dolor e prometre plaer;   10
io, esmaginant, viu sus mi tal poder
que en mon castell era esclau de remença;
io viu un gest e sentí una veu
d'un feble cos, e cuidara jurar
que un armat io el fera congoixar:
sens rompre'm pèl, io em só retut per seu.

Sí com l'infant que sap pel carrer seu
prou bé anar, segons sa poca edat,
si en esculls, per cas, se veu posat,
està pauruc (no sap on se té el peu)   20
d'anar avant, perquè no hi veu petjada;
no vol ne pot usar de camí pla,
tornar no sap, perquè altri el portà,
que ell per si no fera tal jornada.

Mos ulls d'açò han feta la bugada
e tots mos senys s'hi són volguts mesclar;
io pena en pas, mas no hi puc contrastar,
perquè algun tant ab delit és mesclada.
Amor me vol e Fortuna em desvia,
a tals contrasts no basta mon poder;   *over*

No lover can escape the charge of loving little if he remains alive when the one he loves is dead; or he should at least live in retirement from the world and be known only as a hermit.

CI

The Basque who is in Germany, paralysed, unable to make signs, if he is ill, no doctor in the world can cure him, unless he is from Spain; in which case, he will have greater knowledge of his ailment and will understand its nature much better. Thus I (too) find myself in a strange place, so that only you can help me.

I saw a pair of eyes which had such great power to cause suffering and to promise pleasure; I, in my imagination, saw such power exerted over me that in my (own) castle I was a serf; I saw a gesture and heard a voice from a frail body, and I, who would have sworn I was capable of making an armed man suffer, have surrendered to her without receiving a scratch.

Like the child who, for his age, can walk well enough along his own street, but if, by chance, he finds himself among rocks is afraid (he does not know where to set his feet) to go ahead, because he sees no track; he will not and cannot use a level path, he cannot go back since someone else brought him (there), for he would not have come such a way by himself.

My eyes have made a full confession of this, and all my senses have joined in; I suffer because of it, but cannot prevent it, since my suffering is mixed with a little pleasure. Love wants me and Fortune draws me away: my strength is not equal to such conflicts;

sens ella al món remei no puc haver.
(Doncs, dir m'heu vós ja de mi que us paria!)

Dormint, vetlant, io tinc la fantasia
en contemplar qui am, qui és, què val,
e quant més trob, llavors me va pus mal,
pel pensament, qui em met en gran follia;
hoc e en tan gran, que io am son desdeny,
son poc parlar, son estat tal qual és,
més que ésser rei del poble tot francès.
E muira prest, si mon parlar jo em feny!   40

Vós no voler lo meu voler empeny,
e vostres ulls han mon arnès romput;
mon pensament, minvant, m'ha ja vençut;
só presoner, pauruc, per vostre seny.
Lo vostre gest tots mos actes afrena,
e mon voler res no el pot enfrenar;
l'hivern cremant, l'estiu sens escalfar,
aquells perills me daran mala estrena.

Bella ab bon seny, tot és poca faena
al meu afany veure vós lluny estar,   50
car prop de vós res no em pot mal temps dar,
e lluny de vós no trob res bo sens pena.

CV

Puis que sens Tu algú a Tu no basta,
dóna'm la mà o pels cabells me lleva;
si no estenc la mia envers la tua,
quasi forçat a Tu mateix me tira.
Io vull anar envers Tu a l'encontre;
no sé per què no faç lo que volria,
puis io són cert haver voluntat franca
e no sé què aquest voler m'empatxa.

Llevar mi vull e prou no m'hi esforce:
ço fa lo pes de mes terribles colpes;   10
ans que la mort lo procès a mi cloga,
plàcia't, Déu, puis teu vull ser, que ho vulles;   *over*

without her, I can have no hope in this world. (Now you can tell me what you think of my situation!)

Sleeping (and) waking, I engage my imagination in contemplating the person I love, who she is, what she is worth; and the more I find (in her), the worse it is for my thoughts, which lead me to great madness; yes, and so great that I prefer her scorn, her reluctance to speak, her state such as it is, to being king over the entire French nation. And may I die straight away if my words are feigned!

Your lack of love drives on my desire, and your eyes have shattered my armour; my thoughts, weakening (my strength) have already overcome me; I am a prisoner, in fear, of your intelligence. Your gesture restrains all my actions, and nothing can hold back my desire; burning winter, summer without heat: these dangers will give me a poor reward.

Fair and intelligent lady: all tasks are light, (compared) to my trials when I see you far away, for (when I am) near you, nothing can trouble me, and, far from you, I find nothing good without suffering.

CV

Since without you no one reaches you, give me your hand or lift me by the hair; if I do not reach out my hand towards yours, drag me to you by force. I want to go to meet you; I do not know why I do not act as I would wish, since I am certain that my will is free and I do not know what prevents me from this purpose.

I want to rise up and I do not try hard enough: such is the weight of my terrible sins; before death puts an end to my suit, may it please you, God, since I wish to be yours, to wish it also;

fes que ta sang mon cor dur amollesca:
de semblant mal guarí ella molts altres.
Ja lo tardar ta ira em denuncia;
ta pietat no troba en mi què obre.

Tan clarament en l'entendre no peque
com lo voler he carregat de colpa.
Ajuda'm Déu! Mas follament te pregue,
car Tu no vals sinó al qui s'ajuda,   20
e tots aquells qui a Tu se apleguen,
no els pots fallir, e mostren-ho tos braços.
¿ Què faré io, que no meresc m'ajudes,
car tant com puc conec que no m'esforce ?

Perdona mi si follament te parle!
De passió parteixen mes paraules.
Io sent paor d'infern, al qual faç via;
girar-la vull, e no hi disponc mos passos.
Mas io em record que meretist lo Lladre
(tant quant hom veu no hi bastaven ses obres);   30
ton esperit lla on li plau espira;
com ne per què no sap qui en carn visca.

Ab tot que só mal crestià per obra,
ira no et tinc ne de res no t'incolpe;
io són tot cert que per tostemps bé obres,
e fas tant bé donant mort com la vida:
tot és egual quant surt de ta potença,
d'on tinc per foll qui vers Tu es vol irèixer.
Amor de mal, e de bé ignorança,
és la raó que els hòmens no et coneixen.   40

A Tu deman que lo cor m'enfortesques,
sí que el voler ab ta voluntat lligue;
e puis que sé que lo món no em profita,
dóna'm esforç que del tot l'abandone,
e lo delit que el bon hom de Tu gusta,
fes-me'n sentir una poca centilla,
perquè ma carn, qui m'està molt rebel.le,
haja afalac, que del tot no em contraste.   *over*

make your blood soften my hard heart: it has cured many others of a similar affliction. Already your anger accuses my delay; your pity finds nothing in me to work upon.

I do not sin so clearly in my understanding as I have burdened my will with guilt. Help me, God! But I pray to you foolishly, since you only help the man who helps himself, and you cannot fail any who approach you, and your arms are a sign of this. What am I to do, since I do not deserve your help, for I know that I do not make as much effort as I might.

Forgive me if I speak to you foolishly! My words come from suffering. I fear Hell, towards which I travel; I want to go back, and do not turn my steps in that direction. But I remember that you rewarded the thief (as far as one can see, his works were not sufficient); your spirit breathes where it pleases; how or why, no living man knows.

Though I am a bad Christian in my works, I am not angry with you nor do I blame you in any way; I am quite certain that you continually perform good and (that) you are right whether you give death or life: everything is equal when it comes from your power, so that I consider anyone a fool who is angry with you. Love of evil and ignorance of good is the reason men do not know you.

I beg you to strengthen my heart so that my will may be joined with yours; and, since I know that the world is of no profit to me, give me strength to reject it altogether and let me feel a tiny spark of the pleasure which the good man enjoys in you, so that my flesh, which rebels so much against me, may be appeased and not wholly contrary to me.

Ajuda'm, Déu, que sens Tu no em puc moure,
perquè el meu cos és més que paralític!   50
Tant són en mi envellits los mals hàbits,
que la virtut al gustar m'és amarga.
Oh Déu, mercè! Revolta'm ma natura,
que mala és per la mia gran colpa;
e si per mort io puc rembre ma falta,
esta serà ma dolça penitença.

Io tem a Tu més que no et só amable,
e davant Tu confés la colpa aquesta;
torbada és la mia esperança,
e dintre mi sent terrible baralla.   60
Io veig a Tu just e misericorde;
veig ton voler qui sens mèrits gracia;
dónes e tols de grat lo do sens mèrits.
Qual és tan just, quant més io, que no tema?

Si Job lo just por de Déu l'opremia,
què faré io que dins les colpes nade?
Com pens d'infern que temps no s'hi esmenta,
lla és mostrat tot quant sentiments temen.
L'arma, qui és contemplar Déu eleta,
encontra Aquell, blasfemant, se rebel.la;   70
no és en hom de tan gran mal estima.
Doncs, ¿com està qui vers tal part camina?

Prec-te, Senyor, que la vida m'abreuges
ans que pejors casos a mi enseguesquen;
en dolor visc faent vida perversa,
e tem dellà la mort per tostemps llonga.
Doncs, mal deçà, e dellà mal sens terme.
Pren-me al punt que millor en mi trobes;
lo detardar no sé a què em servesca;
no té repòs lo qui té fer viatge.   80

Io em dolc perquè tant com vull no em puc dolre
de l'infinit damnatge, lo qual dubte;
e tal dolor no la recull natura,
ne es pot asmar, e menys sentir pot l'home.   *over*

Help me, God, for I cannot move without you, since my body is worse than paralysed! Evil habits have grown so old in me that I find virtue bitter to the taste. O mercy, God! Reverse my nature, which is evil because of my great sin; and if by death I can redeem my error, this will be my sweet penitence.

I fear, rather than love, you, and in your presence I confess this sin: my hope is troubled and I feel great discord within me. I see you (to be) just and merciful; I see your will which grants grace without merits; you freely give and take away your gift without merits. What man is so just, let alone myself, that he is not afraid?

If Job, the just (man), was oppressed by fear of God, what shall I do, who swim in sins? When I think of Hell, where time is of no account, there all that the feelings fear is manifest. The soul, which was chosen to contemplate God, rebels, blaspheming, against Him; man cannot reckon such great evil. Then what is the state of the man who travels in that direction?

I beg you, Lord, to cut short my life before worse things happen to me; I live in pain, leading a perverse life, and I fear everlasting death in the next world. Then, evil here and evil afterwards, without end. Take me when you consider me most ready; I do not know what use there is to me in delaying; there is no rest for a man who is to go on a journey.

I grieve because I cannot grieve as much as I should like at the infinite damnation which I fear; and nature does not comprehend such suffering, nor can man appreciate, still less feel, it.

E, doncs, açò sembla a mi flaca excusa,
com de mon dan, tant com és, no m'espante;
si el cel deman, no li dó basta estima;
fretura pas de por e d'esperança.

Per bé que Tu irascible t'amostres,
ço és defalt de nostra ignorança;   90
lo teu voler tostemps guarda clemença,
ton semblant mal és bé inestimable.
Perdona'm, Déu, si t'he donada colpa,
car io confés ésser aquell colpable;
ab ull de carn he fets los teus judicis:
vulles dar llum a la vista de l'arma!

Lo meu voler al teu és molt contrari,
e em só enemic pensant-me amic ésser.
Ajuda'm, Déu, puis me veus en tal pressa!
Io em desesper, si los mèrits meus guardes;   100
io m'enuig molt la vida com allongue,
e dubte molt que aquella fenesca;
en dolor visc, car mon desig no es ferma,
e ja en mi alterat és l'arbitre.

Tu est la fi on totes fins termenen,
e no és fi, si en Tu no termena;
Tu est lo bé on tot altre es mesura,
e no és bo qui a Tu, Déu, no sembla.
Al qui et complau, Tu, aquell, déu nomenes;
per Tu semblar, major grau d'home el muntes;   110
d'on és gran dret del qui plau al diable,
prenga lo nom d'aquell ab qui es conforma.

Alguna fi en aquest món se troba;
no és vera fi, puis que no fa l'hom fèlix;
és lo començ per on altra s'acaba,
segons lo córs que entendre pot un home.
Los filosofs qui aquella posaren
en si mateix, són ésser vists discordes:
senyal és cert que en veritat no es funda;
per conseqüent, a l'home no contenta.   *over*

And yet this seems to me a poor excuse, that I am not afraid of my corruption, great as it is; if I ask for Heaven, I do not value it sufficiently; I am lacking in both fear and hope.

Though you show yourself (to be) angry, this is the fault of our ignorance; your will continually displays clemency, your hostile appearance is immeasurably good. Forgive me, God, if I have thought you to blame, for I confess that I am the one at fault; I have judged you with an eye of flesh: I beg you give light to the eyes of the soul!

My will is quite contrary to your own, and I am an enemy to myself when I think to be a friend. Help me, God, since you see me in such a strait! I despair if you consider my desserts; I am greatly vexed that my life should be drawn out, and I am terrified that it may end; I live in suffering, for my desire is not firm and my judgement is now disturbed in me.

You are the end in which all ends terminate, and it is not an end if it does not end in you. You are the good which is the measure of all other goods, and he who does not resemble you, God, is not good. Him who pleases you, you call a god; for, resembling you, you raise him to a higher level than man; therefore it is very right that he who pleases the devil should take the name of him with whom he conforms.

Any end (which is) found in this world is not a true end, since it does not make men happy; it is the beginning through which another end is achieved, according to the process one may understand. Those philosophers who placed the true end in oneself are seen (to be) in disagreement: this is a sure sign that it is not based on truth; consequently, it is of no satisfaction to man.

Bona per si no fón la llei judaica
(en paradís per ella no s'entrava),
mas tant com fón començ d'aquesta nostra,
de què es pot dir d'aquestes dues una.
Així la fi de tot en tot humana
no da repòs a l'apetit o terme,
mas tampoc l'hom sens ella no ha l'altra:
sent Joan fón senyalant lo Messies.

No té repòs qui nulla altra fi guarda,
car en res àls lo voler no reposa;   130
ço sent cascú, e no hi cal subtilesa,
que fora Tu lo voler no s'atura.
Sí com los rius a la mar tots acorren,
així les fins totes en Tu se n'entren.
Puis te conec, esforça'm que io t'ame!
Vença l'amor a la por que io et porte!

E si amor tanta com vull no m'entra,
creix-me la por, sí que, tement, no peque,
car, no pecant, io perdré aquells hàbits
que són estats, perquè no t'am, la causa.   140
Muiren aquells qui de Tu m'apartaren,
puis m'han mig mort e em tolen que no visca.
Oh senyor Déu! Fes que la vida em llargue,
puis me apar que envers Tu io m'acoste.

¿Qui em mostrarà davant Tu fer excusa,
quan hauré dar mon mal ordenat compte?
Tu m'has donat disposició recta,
e io he fet del regle falç molt corba.
Dreçar-la vull, mas he mester ta ajuda.
Ajuda'm, Déu, car ma força és flaca;   150
desig saber què de mi predestines:
a Tu és present i a mi causa venible.

No et prec que em dóns sanitat de persona
ne béns alguns de natura i fortuna,
mas solament que a Tu, Déu, sols ame,
car io só cert que el major bé s'hi causa.   *over*

The Mosaic law was not good in itself (one could not enter Paradise by means of it), except insofar as it was the beginning of our own law, because of which it can be said that the laws are a single one. Thus the wholly human end gives no rest or term to the appetite, though without it man does not achieve the other: Saint John announced the coming of the Messiah.

He who considers a different end has no rest, for the will does not rest in any other thing; all men feel this, and it requires no subtlety, for outside yourself the will does not rest. Just as all rivers run to the sea, so all ends enter into you. Since I know you, give me the strength to love you! Let love overcome the fear I have of you!

And if love does not enter into me as I should wish, increase my fear, so that, fearing, I may not sin; for, by not sinning, I shall lose those habits which have been the cause of my not loving you. Let those habits which kept me from you die, since they have half killed me and taken away my life. O Lord God! Prolong my life, since I feel I am drawing near to you.

Who will show me how to make excuses before you, when I have to give a detailed account of my sins? You have given me a straight commandment, and I have made this rule into a bent sickle. I want to straighten it, but I need your help. Help me, God, for my strength is weak; I desire to know what you have predestined for me; to you, it is present, and to me, a future cause.

I do not ask you to give me physical health or any goods of nature or fortune, but merely, God, to make me love you, for I am certain that the greatest good derives from this.

Per conseqüent, delectació alta
io no la sent, per no dispost sentir-la;
mas per saber, un home grosser jutja
que el major bé sus tots és delitable.   160

Qual serà el jorn que la mort io no tema?
E serà quan de ta amor io m'inflame,
e no es pot fer sens menyspreu de la vida,
e que per Tu aquella io menyspree.
Lladoncs seran jus mi totes les coses
que de present me veig sobre los muscles;
lo qui no tem del fort lleó les ungles,
molt menys tembrà lo fibló de la vespa.

Prec-te, Senyor, que em faces insensible
e que en null temps alguns delits io senta,   170
no solament los lleigs qui et vénen contra,
mas tots aquells que indiferents se troben.
Açò desig perquè sol en Tu pense
e pusca haver la via que en Tu es dreça;
fes-ho, Senyor, e si per temps me'n torne,
haja per cert trobar ta aurella sorda.

Tol-me dolor com me veig perdre el segle,
car mentre em dolc, tant com vull io no t'ame,
e vull-ho fer, mas l'hàbit me contrasta;
en temps passat me carreguí la colpa.   180
Tant te cost io com molts qui no et serviren,
e Tu els has fet no menys que io et demane;
per què et suplic que dins lo cor Tu m'entres,
puix est entrat en pus abominable.

Catòlic só, mas la Fe no m'escalfa,
que la fredor lenta dels senys apaga,
car io lleix ço que mos sentiments senten,
e paradís crec per fe i raó jutge.
Aquella part de l'esperit és prompta,
mas la dels senys rossegant-la'm acoste;   190
doncs Tu, Senyor, al foc de fe m'acorre,
tant que la part que em porta fred, abrase.

over

Consequently, I do not feel great delight, since I am not disposed to feel it; but, through his knowledge, a coarse man reckons that the greatest good is delightful above all others.

When will be the day I no longer fear death ? It will be when I am set on fire by your love, and that cannot be without contempt for life and without my despising it for your sake. Then all those things will be beneath me which at present weigh upon my sinews; he who is not afraid of the claws of the strong lion will fear much less the sting of the wasp.

I beg you, Lord, to make me unfeeling, so that I never again experience any pleasures: not only those base pleasures which attack one, but all those which are indifferent. I desire this so that I may think only of you and may find the way which leads towards you; do this, Lord, and if I ever stray from it, may I be sure to find your ear deaf.

Take away the anguish of seeing myself lose the world, for as long as I grieve (for it) I do not love you as much as I would, and I wish to do this, but custom hinders me; in time past I loaded myself with sin. I am worth as much to you as many who never served you, and you have done no less for them than I ask of you; and so I beg you to enter my heart, since you have entered other more wretched ones.

I am a Catholic, but Faith does not warm me, for the slow cold of the senses puts (it) out, since I leave all that my emotions feel, and believe in Paradise by faith and judge it by reason. The spiritual part of me is ready, but I draw near dragging behind me my sensual part. Then help me, Lord, with the fire of faith, and consume in fire that part of me which is cold.

Tu creïst mé perquè l'ànima salve,
e pot-se fer de mi saps lo contrari.
Si és així, ¿ per què, doncs, me creaves
puix fón en Tu lo saber infal.lible ?
Torn a no-res, io et suplic, lo meu ésser,
car més me val que tostemps l'escur càrcer;
io crec a Tu com volguist dir de Judes
que el fóra bo no fos nat al món home.   200

Per mi segur, havent rebut baptisme,
no fos tornat als braços de la vida,
mas a la mort hagués retut lo deute
e de present io no viuria en dubte !
Major dolor d'infern los hòmens senten
que los delits de paraís no jutgen;
lo mal sentit és d'aquell altre exemple,
e paradís sens lo sentir se jutja.

Dóna'm esforç que prenga de mi venja.
Io em trob ofès contra Tu ab gran colpa,   210
e si no hi bast, Tu de ma carn te farta,
ab què no em tocs l'esperit, que a Tu sembla;
e sobretot ma fe que no vacil.le
e no tremol la mia esperança;
no em fallirà caritat, elles fermes,
e de la carn, si et suplic, no me n'oges.

Oh, quan serà que regaré les galtes
d'aigua de plor ab les llàgremes dolces !
Contricció és la font d'on emanen:
aquesta és la clau que el cel tancat nos obre.   220
D'atricció parteixen les amargues,
perquè en temor més en amor se funden;
mas, tals quals són, d'aquestes me abunda,
puix són camí e via per les altres.

You created me that I might save my soul, and you know that the reverse may happen to me. If this is so, why, then, did you create me, since your knowledge was infallible? Change into nothingness, I pray, my being, for I prefer that to the dark, everlasting prison. I believe, as you chose to say of Judas, that it would have been better for him not to have been born a man.

It would have been as well for me if, having received baptism, I had not returned to the arms of life, but had then paid my account to death, so that now I would not be living in doubt! Men fear the pains of Hell more than they appreciate the joys of Paradise; another example of this is the evil which we feel, whereas we think of Paradise without feeling it.

Give me the strength to take vengeance upon myself. I find I have offended you with great sin; and if I am too weak, gorge yourself on my flesh, but do not touch my spirit, which resembles you; and, above all, may my faith not wander nor my hope tremble; charity will not fail me if they are firm, and if I pray to you for my flesh, do not listen to me.

Oh, when shall I water my cheeks with the sweet tears of weeping? Contrition is the spring from which they flow: this is the key which opens the gates of Heaven for us. Bitter (tears) come from attrition, since they arise from fear rather than love; but, even as they are, give me abundance of these, since they are the path and way to the others.

CXIV

Retinga'm Déu en mon trist pensament,
puis que no em tol ço per què pas tristor!
En ella sent una tan gran dolçor
per si, e com altre delit no sent,
sens grat seré si jamés la'm despull,
e solament assaig d'ella eixir.
Tan gran delit me sent d'ella venir
que no desig res fora mi, ni vull.

Tot quant io pense e tot quant veu mon ull,
tant com és bell e m'és portant delit,   10
de tant me trob io pus adolorit,
car en mon cor bon delit no es recull.
Fet és de mi lo que es devia fer.
Perdent Amor, no vull que m'ajut Déu
en fer que el món me done res del seu,
puis no té res dispost a mon voler.

Menys de ser trist, no em plau delit haver:
d'aquell ho dic, ab la tristor mesclat,
car aquest és lo pus terrible estat
de tots aquells que es pot al món saber.   20
Io perd açò que molt hom ha perdut,
e me'n dolc més, tant com d'amor los pas.
Per massa amar io em trob en aquest cas,
no havent àls preat ne conegut.

Amor ha fet que en açò só vengut,
que perd lo món per no poder amar,
e pogra's fer, si pogués comportar
que amàs io e que Amor no m'ajut.
Tot fón ensems veure mi no dispost
e lleixar mé de Amor totalment: 30
de què romanc en tal trist pensament
que a la mort visiblement m'acost.

Trist ab delit, la mort io pendré tost,
e ja en mi és perdut lo remei.
Fort passió abasta mudar llei
e fer d'acer e pedra cor compost.   *over*

CXIV

May God keep me in my sad state of mind, since He does not take away that which makes me sad! In my sadness I feel such great sweetness in itself, and, since I feel no other pleasure, I shall be ungrateful if I ever reject it or even attempt to leave it behind. I feel such great pleasure come from it that I neither desire nor wish for anything outside myself.

All that I think and all that my eye sees, the more beautiful it is and the more pleasure it brings me, the more I find it makes me suffer, for good pleasure does not enter my heart. It is done with me as should be done. Having lost Love, I do not want God to help me by making the world give me anything of its own, since it has nothing to offer to my desire.

I want no pleasure except that of being sad: I mean that pleasure (which is) mixed with sadness, for this is the most terrible condition of all those which can be known on earth. I am losing what many men have lost, and I suffer more, the more I excel them in love. Through loving to excess, I find myself in this situation, not having wished for or known anything else.

Love has made me come to this: that I lose the world through being unable to love; and perhaps I *might* love, if he would allow me to love without his help. At one and the same time, I found myself disinclined and totally abandoned by love: because of which, I remain in such a sad state of mind that I visibly draw near to death.

Sad with pleasure, I shall soon come to die and all hope of cure is now lost to me. Great suffering can alter the law and make a heart composed of steel and stone.

Io sóc aquest que en la mort delit prenc,
puis que no tolc la causa per què em ve.
Ma passió en tristor me deté,
que no sent pus en son temps ni entenc.   40

Mon mal no és tant com en altre en venc:
io l'he fet gran, preant molt lo que perd,
car, veent mé de tota amor desert,
la terra em fall e al cel no m'estenc.
Mentre no pens, io trob algun repòs,
mes l'esperit meu tostemps està trist
per l'hàbit pres, que llong temps és que vist,
d'un negre drap o celici molt gros.

No em fa delit res pertanyent al cos,
puis l'esperit no hi és participant.   50
Natura en mi sàviament obrant
vol que m'esforç e mon dret no hi pos;
e, ja del tot vençut per l'hàbit vell,
no prenc delit en res fora el costum.
Pensant mos mals, tot lo temps hi consum,
essent-hi bé, puis me delit en ell.

No trob en mi voler e menys consell
a desijar cosa alguna del món.
Mos pensaments recollits dins mi són,
per no pensar res que sia d'aquell.   60
Lo dia clar voldria fos escur,
udolaments e plors en lloc de cants.
No té lo món coses a mi bastants
a fer que dol per tostemps no m'atur.

Per ignorar ve que l'hom se procur
grossos delits, no sabent quant se nou.
Fora tot seny és qui sos comptes clou,
que, perduts ells, del món se desnatur.
Açò és ver, mas tristor me té pres
tant que delit sent com tal me conec,   70
e sap fer tant que tot delit renec,
ne puc sentir altre en senta jamés.   *over*

I am this man who takes pleasure in death, since I do not avoid the reason for which it comes to me. My suffering keeps me in sadness, so that, while it lasts, I cease to feel or understand.

My misfortune is not as great as that which occurred to others: I have made it great by valuing highly what I lose; for, seeing myself deprived of all love, earth fails me and I cannot reach to Heaven. As long as I do not think, I find some rest, but my spirit is continually sad because of the kind of dress it has adopted, (and) which for a long time it has worn, of black material or coarse sackcloth.

Nothing which concerns the body gives me pleasure, since the spirit has no part in it. Nature, acting wisely in me, wants me to make an effort, and I do not apply myself to this (as I should); and now, entirely overcome by my old habits, I take no pleasure in unfamiliar things. I spend my whole time thinking of my misfortunes, and am at ease in this, since I find pleasure in it.

I find in myself neither desire nor yet guidance to wish for anything on earth; my thoughts are gathered within me, so as not to think of anything to do with the world. I wish the clear day were dark, (and that there were) howls and tears instead of songs. There is nothing on earth sufficient to dissuade me from remaining forever in mourning.

It is through ignorance that man seeks gross pleasures, not realizing how much harm he does to himself. He is out of his senses who settles his accounts and, in losing such pleasures, is divorced from human nature. This is true, but sadness has taken hold of me, so that I feel joy at seeing myself in this state, and it can compel me to renounce all pleasure: nor can I think that I might feel pleasure again.

Molts han jaquit lo món sens perdre res,
mas per consell de llur bona raó,
e io el jaquesc per falsa opinió,
pensant que perd lo món e tot quant és.
Mon foll pensar me disponc voler tal
que ha fet mi déu d'Amor adorar,
e io forçat de aquell apartar,
me par ser bo tot quant a tots és mal.   80

Puis que lo món ni Déu a mi no val
a rellevar la causa d'on só trist,
a mi plau bé la tristor que io vist;
delit hi sent, mentre io em trobe tal.
Així dispost, dolç me sembla l'amarg,
tant és en mi infeccionat lo gust!
A temps he cor d'acer, de carn e fust.
Io só aquest que em dic Ausias March!

A Déu suplic que el viure no m'allarg,
o meta en mi aquest propòsit ferm: 90
que mon voler envers Ell lo referm,
perquè, anant a Ell, no trobe embarg.

Many have left the world without losing anything, following the advice of their good reason; and I leave it through false opinion, thinking I lose the world and all that is (in it). My foolish thoughts placed such a desire in me as has made me worship the god of Love, and, now I am compelled to leave him, what to others is evil to me seems good.

Since neither the world nor God helps me to root out the reason for which I am sad, I am content with the sadness I wear; I feel joy, while I am in such a state. Thus disposed, what is bitter seems sweet to me: so corrupted is my taste! I have a heart of steel, flesh and wood, all in one. I am this man who is called Ausias March!

I pray God not to prolong my life, or (else) to instil in me this firm intention: to strengthen my will towards Him, so that, travelling towards Him, I shall meet with no obstacles.

Notes to the Poems

I   [p. *28*]

Basically, this poem is a set of variations on a well-known passage from Boethius: 'But this is that which vexeth me most, when I remember it. For in all adversity of fortune it is the most unhappy kind of misfortune to have been happy' (*Consolation of Philosophy* II, iv). In the *Divine Comedy*, Dante compresses this thought into a single memorable phrase: 'Nessun maggior dolore / che ricordarsi del tempo felice / nella miseria . . .' (*Inferno* V, 121–3). Ausias March, characteristically, expands it into a series of similes.

41–44. As often in March, the *tornada* or *envoi* is virtually independent of the rest of the poem. As Bohigas observes: '(Such endings) are like brief epigrams in which the poet casts aside conventional modes of expression and concentrates his own experience' (II, 8).

41. *Plena de seny*: literally, 'Full of sense', though *seny* here is a complex word implying not only reasonableness, but intelligence and skill in the more spiritual aspects of courtly love. A similar concept of 'intelligence' is assumed by Dante in the First *Canzone* of the *Vita Nuova*: 'Donne, ch'avete intelletto d'amore. . . .'

44. *creurà:* literally, 'he will believe'. Some texts have the infinitive form *creure* ('to believe'), but this hardly seems to fit the syntax.

II   [p. *30*]

6. *incomportable*: literally, 'unbearable'.

11–12. *e cella clau . . . portal*: Early locks were sometimes so complicated that they required two keys, one to open, the other to shut them.

17–18. *Menys que lo peix . . . han llur sojorn*: perhaps a reminiscence of Virgil, *Eclogue* I, 59–60 ('Ante leves ergo pascentur in aethere cervi/et freta destituent nudos in litore pisces'), though the figure is a commonplace in medieval writing.

34. *qualitat*: here, 'the spiritual'. In other poems, *quantitat* ('quantity') is used to indicate material things.

III [p. *32*]

1. *Alt*: strictly speaking, 'satisfaction', 'liking'. The sequence here is quite rigorous: 'liking' and 'love' precede 'desire'; the three emotions together give rise to hope.

5. *sens fum continu foc*: The reference is to the hidden fire of love. In the medical simile of the second stanza, this state is compared by implication with that of a sick man whose disease does not affect the temperature of his skin.

20. *cella*: The feminine form of the demonstrative implies *causa* or *raó* ('reason').

IV [p. *34*]

7. *dues dones*: This phrase has sometimes been taken allegorically to mean the bodily and spiritual aspects of the same woman. However, there seems no reason why it should not be understood literally.

9–10. *Sí com la mar . . . egualment*: Cf. Dante, *Inferno* V, 28–30: 'Io venni in loco d'ogni luce muto, / che mugghia come fa mar per tempesta / se da contrari venti é combattuto'.

34. *prim moviment*: The first, or prime, impulse comes from the senses, which then awaken the understanding. The psychological process described in this passage resembles the action of the winds in stanza two.

47. *volenterós acte de bé és dit*: The notion of love as an act of the will is scholastic. Cf. Aquinas: 'to love a person is to will good for that person' (*Summa Theologica Ia*, 20, 1).

X [p. *38*]

4. *sobrats*: = *sobrat*. The -*s* ending in a singular noun or adjective is a relic of Provençal usage, employed here to complete the rhyme. Cf. *ignocents* in line 43.

23. *los tres poders*: the three powers of the soul, i.e. memory, understanding and will. As the rest of the poem makes clear, it is the power of memory which the speaker has forfeited.

35. *alguatzir*: originally, 'vizier'; by extension, 'governor' or anyone appointed to carry out the orders of a superior authority.

XI [p. *40*]

25. *Bé em meravell com és tan ergullosa*: There is a break in the structure here: instead of applying the allegory of the opening, the speaker goes on to describe his own situation as a lover.

31. *acolorat:* literally, 'disguised in false colours'.

38. *l'humit*: i.e. the blood.

42. *civilment*: The implication is 'socially', 'as a citizen'.

XIII [p. *42*]

9. *Cascú requer e vol a son semblant*: The notion that like seeks like occurs in both Aristotle and Aquinas. Cf. *Summa Theologica Ia, IIae*, 8, 1: 'every inclination is to something like and suitable

to the thing inclined'.

13. *Lo rei xipré*: Janus de Lusignan, who was captured at the Battle of Chierochitia (7 July 1426) and taken to Cairo, where he remained until his release in May 1427. The dates are of interest for the composition of the poem, since March speaks of the event as if it were topical.

17. *Teixion*: In Greek mythology, Tityos was a giant whose entrails were devoured by a vulture and continually renewed. Dante refers to him in *Inferno* XXXI, 124.

24. *cǫ que*: i.e. the fulfilment of love.

XVIII   [p. *46*]

11. *qui els*: = *en els quals*. The suppression of prepositions is frequent in Ausias March. See Bohigas V, 196–7.

30. *Amor minva*: The verb here is intransitive; literally, 'Love decreases'.

41–44. *Pren-me enaixí . . . torbassen*: The philosopher in question is probably Crates the Cynic. Aquinas (*Summa Theologica* IIa, IIae, 186, 3) quotes a similar anecdote from St Jerome.

XIX   [p. *48*]

17. *mon esperdiment*: literally, 'my perdition'.

24. *l'avorrit camí*: i.e. the road to death.

XXIII   [p. *52*]

1. *l'estil dels trobadors*: 'manner', rather than 'style' in a literary sense. See Introduction, p. 8.

28. *Dona Teresa*: This is the only poem in which the woman addressed is actually named. The identification with Teresa Bou, a hypothetical member of a family known to have existed in Valencia at the time March was writing, was first made by Lluís Carrós de Vilaragut in 1546. Though many subsequent biographers have accepted this claim, no firm evidence for it has yet come to light.

44. *Lla on miracle està*: Dante also refers to the 'miraculous' beauty of his lady in Sonnet XV of the *Vita Nuova*: 'E par che sia una cosa venuta / di cielo in terra a miracol mostrare'.

XXXIX   [p. *54*]

As Bohigas observes (II, 135), this poem comes closer than most to the spirit and diction of the troubadours, though one cannot point to any specific influences.

18. *d'Amor les festes colre*: i.e. as if Love were a saint.

XLVI   [p. *58*]

3–6. *Mestre i Ponent . . . Tramuntanal*: A good deal of the flavour of these lines comes from March's use of familiar seamen's terms for the various Mediterranean winds. The mistral and the tramontana blow respectively from the north and the north-west.

9. *Bullirà el mar com la cassola en forn*: a powerful rendering of

Job XLI, 31, which in the Vulgate reads: 'Fervescere faciet quasi ollam profundum mare'.

25. *Io tem la mort per no ser-vos absent*: Cf. XIII, line 25 et seq.

26–27. *anul.lats . . . sobrats*: These are both singular forms. See note to X, line 4.

34. *tost*: Bohigas adopts the alternative reading *tots* which appears in a number of MSS. *Tots* ('all')—a singular form with an -*s* ending—would imply that, after the speaker's death, the lady's whole power to love might turn to hate.

38. *aquell*: refers back to *terme*, i.e. 'that I might have come to that limit . . .'.

LXIII [p. *64*]

59–60. *calor . . . radical*: In medieval medicine, 'radical heat' refers to the heat which is naturally inherent in all animals and human beings, its presence forming a necessary condition of their vitality.

LXVI [p. *68*]

41–42. *lo jorn que l'Ignocent . . . en lo pal*: one of the few possible reminiscences of Petrarch in Ausias March. Both poets claim to have fallen in love on Good Friday. Cf. Petrarch, Sonnet XXXIV: 'Era il giorno ch'al sol si scoloraro / per la pietà del suo fattore i rai, / quando i' fui preso, . . .'.

LXVIII [p. *70*]

1–8. *No em pren així . . . en major*: As Pagès points out (*A. M. et ses prédécesseurs*, 35–37), this stanza is a direct imitation of a passage from the troubadour poet Peire Ramon de Tolosa, beginning: 'Si com l'enfans qu'es alevatz petitz / en cort valen et honratz del seingor . . .'

9–16. *¿ Com se farà . . . millor festa*: This stanza does not appear in the early editions, and was published for the first time in 1555. However, there are no strong reasons for doubting its authenticity: metrically, it is necessary in order to preserve the overall rhyme scheme of the poem; from the point of view of sense, the reflections it contains both prolong and complete the simile of the first stanza.

21. *senyor*: i.e. Love, who has always been his own master.

LXXIII [p. *72*]

58. *tres parts*: Love has three parts or aspects: one is mortal, another eternal; the third corresponds to 'false appetite'.

LXXVII [p. *76*]

25–28. *Amor, Amor . . . és posat*: These lines were imitated by the Castilian poet Garcilaso de la Vega (1501 ?–36) in the opening quatrain of Sonnet XXVII: 'Amor, Amor, un hábito vestí / el cual de vuestro paño fue cortado; / al vestir ancho fue, mas apretado / y estrecho cuando estuvo sobre mí'.

LXXIX   [p. *78*]

9. *per tres calitats*: The allegory of the arrows of Love has
earlier medieval precedents. Of the three kinds—gold, silver,
lead—only the first is mortal. March's description is based on
some lines from a poem by the troubadour poet Guiraut de
Calansó, 'A leis cui am de cor e de saber. . .'. Cf. Bohigas III,
123–4.

30. *anar en cabells*: i.e. without a helmet for protection.

LXXXIX   [p. *82*]

1. *Cervo ferit no desija la font*: Cf. Psalm XLII, 1: 'As the hart
panteth after the water brooks, so panteth my soul after thee, O
God'.

24. *al poc estat no par l'ofensa greu*: The metaphor here refers to
the accepted social hierarchy of the time. An offence committed
against a member of the lower orders is less serious than one
committed against a member of the nobility; similarly, the injury
done to the speaker by his lady's disdain will be in proportion to
the excellence of his love.

39. *d'amor haveu haver forçat consell*: literally, 'you must have
love's obligatory counsel'.

51–52. *de vostre cos . . . ne em fos altiu*: These lines seem to
suggest that the woman is incapable of going beyond sensual
love; hence the speaker's mistrust in line 49.

XCII   [p. *84*]

This is the first of the group of six poems (XCII–XCVII) generally
known as the *Cants de Mort* or 'Songs of Death'.

1. *Aquelles mans*: i.e. the hands of Atropos, of the three Fates in
Greek mythology, the one who cuts the thread of life.

13–14. *quantitat . . . qualitat*: See note to II, line 34.

19. *los sants amants*: not Love's martyrs, as has sometimes been
supposed, but those who have loved with 'honest love'.

36. *cataracte*: 'Honest love' gives sight to blind passion, but this
sight is only partial: it cannot remove the 'cataract' entirely.

38. *gota serena*: amaurosis, the weakening of the optical nerve.

43. *l'altre*: i.e. love which involves both body and spirit, like
the 'desires' referred to in line 49 and the 'other desire' of line 55.

54. *vitals letovaris*: singular forms, despite the -*s* endings. See
note to X, line 4.

72. *mes natures*: The plural implies both bodily and spiritual
natures. Cf. lines 201–4.

75. *Aquell voler*: This 'human' love, described in lines 81–90,
is both physical and spiritual.

77. *l'extrem d'aquest*: The ultimate refinement of 'human' love
is the pure union of spirits. The 'worm' here, as in I, line 42, is a
symbol of absence.

79–80. *Opinió falsa . . . habita*: The speaker is arguing that, contrary to common opinion, the 'human' love which he is describing exists both within and outside us, and thus shares in both matter and spirit.

89. *aquesta amor*: Love which is merely physical, and consequently lacking in truth, does not experience the conflicts between the physical and spiritual natures involved in 'human' love.

150. *comparat*: = *comparable*. One would normally expect the preposition *a* (*al diable*). See note to XVIII, line 11.

179. *la muller aimia*: On the possible ambiguity of this expression, see Introduction, p. 18.

210. *lo bo*: i.e. pure love.

216. *los composts*: For March, as for Aquinas, all human actions reflect the compound, or dual, nature of man. His use of the word *compost* resembles Aquinas's own use of the terms 'compositus' and 'conjunctus'; e.g. *Summa Theologica* 1a, 11ae, 74, 4: 'It is clear that man is not so much soul as something composed ("compositum") of soul and body'. For a good account of Aquinas's theories concerning the relationship between body and soul, see F. C. Copleston, *Aquinas* (Harmondsworth 1955), Chapter IV.

247–48. *Ferí'ls Amor . . . els veïne*: These lines are composed in the manner of an epitaph. This tone is maintained to the end of the poem, though in the last two lines March modulates very skilfully into the first person plural.

XCIV [p. *98*]

The third of the *Cants de Mort*.

12–13. *quantitat . . . qualitat*: See note to 11, line 34.

17. *humors*: Medieval physiologists, following Galen, believed that individual temperament was determined by the varying proportions of the four humours, or vital juices: blood, choler, melancholy and phlegm.

23–24. *per ella es fan los actes . . . la causa*: i.e. the soul is the agent of acts whose cause derives from the body.

30. *contrassemble*: = 'corresponding', 'equal in quality, in moral or social value'.

33. *Dos volers*: reason and appetite, as line 37 makes clear.

51. *L'altre voler*: i.e. purely spiritual love.

86. *tota carn*: There is a double meaning here: 'all meat', but also 'all flesh'.

XCVI [p. *106*]

The fifth of the *Cants de Mort*.

12. *dubtant estic:* literally, 'I am hesitating'.

21–24. *Si és així . . . adolorit*: For the moral implications of these lines, see Introduction, p. 16.

34. *e tol-ne part*: literally, 'and it derives part of this'.

XCVII [p. *108*]

The sixth and last of the *Cants de Mort*.

17–20. *Enquer està . . . de mi!—*: on the directness of these lines, see Introduction, p. 17.

52. *dull*: an archaic form of *dolc*, used here presumably for the sake of the rhyme.

53. *No bast en més*: literally, 'I do not suffice for more'.

CI [p. *112*]

9–10. *Io viu uns ulls . . .plaer*: These lines are directly imitated from the French poet Alain Chartier (*c.* 1390–*c.* 1440): 'Se onques deux yeulx orent telle puissance / de doner dueil et de prometre joie'.

12. *esclau de remença*: In the social hierarchy of the time, an *esclau de remença* was a serf who had the right to purchase his freedom.

13–16. *io viu un gest . . . per seu*: This is one of the few passages in which Ausias March comes close to Petrarch. Cf. *Trionfi* III, 91–3: 'Ella mi prese, ed io, ch'avrei giurato / difendermi d'un uom coperto d'arme, / con parole e con cenni fui legato . . .'.

25. *han feta la bugada:* Fer *(la) bugada* literally means 'to wash clothes'; here the expression is used figuratively: 'to atone for by weeping'.

39. *del poble tot francès*: Normal syntax would require *de tot el poble francès*.

49. *Bella ab bon seny*: literally, 'Beautiful one with good sense'. On the overtones of *seny*, see note to I, line 41.

CV [p. *114*]

This poem is usually known as the *Cant espiritual* or 'Spiritual Ode'.

13. *fes que ta sang mon cor dur amollesca*: This metaphor refers to the old belief that diamonds, noted for their hardness, could only be made tractable by being immersed in blood.

17–18. *Tan clarament . . . de colpa*: In other words, the speaker has sinned with his will, rather than with his understanding.

22. *e mostren-ho tos braços*: i.e. the outstretched arms of Christ on the Cross.

28. *girar-la vull*: *la* refers to *via*: literally, 'I want to reverse my path'.

31. *on li plau espira*: Cf. *St. John* III, 8: 'The wind bloweth where it listeth'.

67. *que temps no s'hi esmenta*: literally, 'where time is not mentioned'.

80. *té fer*:= *té a fer*. On the suppression of prepositions, see note to XVIII, line 11.

92. *ton semblant mal*: literally, 'that (part) of you which seems bad'.

105–10. *Tu est la fi . . . el muntes*: Notice the change to a more incantatory rhythm.

109. *Tu, aquell, déu nomenes*: Cf. *Psalm* LXXXII, 6: 'I have said, ye are gods'.

117. *Los filosofs*: This is probably no more than a general reference to the sages of antiquity, though the phrase which follows may suggest the Stoics in particular.

121–24. *Bona per si . . . d'aquestes dues una*: This looks back to lines 113–16. The 'two laws' (*dues lleis*) are, of course, the Mosaic and the Christian.

166. *me veig sobre*: literally, 'I see upon'.

189. *Aquella part de l'esperit*: strictly speaking, the 'part' of faith and reason.

199–200. *io crec a Tu . . . home*: Cf. St Matthew XXVI, 24: 'But woe unto that man by whom the Son of Man is betrayed! it had been good for that man if he had not been born'.

219–21. *contricció . . . D'atricció*: Cf. Aquinas, *Summa Theologica* III, suppl. 1, 2, 3,: 'The way of access to perfect contrition is called attrition'.

CXIV   [p. *128*]

47. *per l'hàbit pres*: There is a play on the word *hàbit* here: both 'custom' and 'dress'.

89–92. *A Déu suplic . . . no trobe embarg* In most editions, these four lines are included in the previous stanza and lines 85–8 are transposed to form the *tornada*. Pagès and Bohigas, following the Bibliothèque Nationale MS of 1541, adopt the present order, which, though possibly less dramatic, gives greater coherence to the final stanza.

Bibliography

The following list includes only items that a non-specialist reader may find useful. A fuller bibliography is contained in vol. I of the Bohigas edition, referred to below.

1. EDITIONS AND ANTHOLOGIES

Ausias March, *Obres*, ed. A. Pagès, Institut d'Estudis Catalans (Barcelona 1912–14) 2 vols. The first serious modern edition. Vol. I contains a long critical study of manuscripts, earlier editions, etc.

Ausias March, *Poesies*, ed. P. Bohigas, 'Els nostres clàssics', Barcino (Barcelona 1952–9) 5 vols. The most thorough edition, with good notes to the poems. Vol. I consists of a preliminary study which covers most aspects of March's work.

Ausias March, *Antologia poètica*, ed. J. Fuster, Selecta (Barcelona 1959). Contains modern Catalan versions and a stimulating preface.

M. de Riquer (ed.), *Traducciones castellanas de Ausias March en la Edad de Oro*, Instituto Español de Estudios Mediterráneos (Barcelona 1946). Contains an important preliminary study.

2. CRITICAL STUDIES
    a) in English
G. Brenan, *Literature of the Spanish people*, Penguin Books (Harmondsworth 1963) 253–67.

O. H. Green, *Spain and the Western tradition*, University of Wisconsin (Madison 1963–6) 4 vols. Contains numerous references to Ausias March, mostly in the context of the courtly love tradition.

    b) in French
A. Pagès, *Auzias March et ses prédécesseurs*, École des Hautes Études (Paris 1912).

A. Pagès, *Commentaire des poésies d'Auzias March*, École des Hautes Études (Paris 1935).

    c) in Spanish

M. Menéndez Pelayo, *Antología de poetas líricos castellanos*,
Consejo Superior de Investigaciones Científicas (Madrid 1944–5),
Vol. x, 227–30, 253–67.

R. Lapesa, *La trayectoria poética de Garcilaso*, Revista de
Occidente (Madrid 1948). For influence of Ausias March on
sixteenth-century Spanish poetry.

J. Rubió, 'Literatura catalana', in *Historia general de las
literaturas hispánicas*, Vol. iii, ed. G. Díaz-Plaja, Barna
(Barcelona 1953).

d) in Catalan

M. de Riquer, *Història de la literatura catalana*, Vol. ii, Ariel
(Barcelona 1964) 471–567.

J. Romeu, *Literatura catalana antiga*, Vol. iv, Barcino
(Barcelona 1964) 52–67.

M. de Montoliu, *Ausias March*, Alpha (Barcelona 1959).

J. Rubió, 'Concepte de la poesia en Ausias March', in *De
l'Edat Mitjana al Renaixement*, Aymà (Barcelona 1958) 44–9.

C. Riba, 'Nota a la poesia d'Ausias March', in *Obres completes*,
Vol. ii, Edicions 62 (Barcelona 1967) 485–6.

R. Leveroni, 'Les imatges marines en la poesia d'Ausias
March', *Bulletin of Spanish Studies*, xxviii (1951) 152–66.

P. Ramírez, *La poesia d'Ausias March: anàlisi textual, cronologia,
elements filosòfics*. Ph. D. thesis, University of Basle, privately
printed (Basle 1970).

List of Poems